How Efficiency
Changes the Game

How Efficiency Changes the Game

Developing Lean Operations for Competitive Advantage

Ray Hodge

![BEP logo] BEP

BUSINESS EXPERT PRESS

Leader in applied, concise business books

How Efficiency Changes the Game:
Developing Lean Operations for Competitive Advantage

Copyright © Business Expert Press, LLC, 2021.

Cover design by Charlene Kronstedt

Interior design by Exeter Premedia Services Private Ltd., Chennai, India

First published in 2021 by
Business Expert Press, LLC
222 East 46th Street, New York, NY 10017
www.businessexpertpress.com

ISBN-13: 978-1-63742-044-7 (paperback)
ISBN-13: 978-1-63742-045-4 (e-book)

Business Expert Press Supply and Operations Management Collection

Collection ISSN: 2156-8189 (print)
Collection ISSN: 2156-8200 (electronic)

First edition: 2021

10 9 8 7 6 5 4 3 2 1

Michelle—

Meeting you by chance in the back row of a plane and subsequently proposing to you in the front row, some 12 months later, changed my life. Thank you for your love, belief, and ongoing support.

Description

Obtaining a competitive advantage in today's business environment generally does not happen of its own accord. With the speed of change in technology, products to market, and customer preferences, organizations must strive to keep on the edge and be the drivers of change. Given that most businesses deal with the same buyers in defined markets who purchase similar products, gaining this competitive advantage is critical to both thriving and being leaders in their field. To do this, one must drive efficiencies throughout the entire organization while creating a significant point of difference. Yet, inefficiency continues to run rampant and can be found in the often forgotten pockets of the organization, hampering efficacy at best, leading it out the door at worst.

How Efficiency Changes the Game: Developing Lean Operations for Competitive Advantage provides an insightful process for the executive, manager, and business owner, enabling them to discover inefficiencies where least expected, highlighting both the nature of the primary issues and then how to subsequently correct them. This book will assist in developing lean operations in areas such as leadership, marketing, strategy and planning, sales, time management, workflows, finances, and people.

Keywords

time; process; work; business; sales; change; customer; management; marketing; strategic; efficiency; leadership; competitive advantage; employees; lean

Contents

Foreword

For more than 40 years I have worked with leaders in publicly traded companies, privately held business, and military organizations to help them find the answers to the recurring question: What will help us grow? My answer never varies. It starts with a smart leader with a vision of what the organization can be *tomorrow* rather than what it is *today*. Ray Hodge has taken this observation a step further to offer pragmatic advice about what it takes to create these tomorrows.

Ray understands that a breakthrough product, dazzling service, or cutting-edge technology can put you in the game, but only rock-solid execution of a well-developed strategy can keep you there. You must be able to deliver—to translate your brilliant strategy and operational decisions into action—and you need to do it more efficiently than the competition does.

If you're like many leaders, however, in an effort to improve performance, too frequently you address the *symptoms* of dysfunction, not the root causes of it. You focus your attention and that of others on what's going wrong instead of *why* it doesn't work.

As Ray points out, it all starts with a strong strategic principle—a shared objective about what the organization wants to accomplish. Clear strategy leads the process; great performance completes it. However, the two should not be confused. *Strategy* is an over- and misused term to describe anything important, and *strategic planning* is an oxymoron. Leaders *formulate* the strategy; they *plan* the execution—or at least the successful ones do. Execution involves discipline; it requires senior leader involvement; and it should be central to the organization's culture. Done well, execution pushes everyone to decipher their broad-brush theoretical understanding of the strategy into intimate familiarity with how it will work, who will take charge of it, how long it will take, how much it will cost, and how it will affect the organization overall.

Effective tactics form the foundation of execution, but the two differ. Tactics are the *activities* that lead to execution, but by themselves, they aren't enough. Execution shapes strategy, and strategy defines execution. Strategy formulation involves asking "What?" Execution is a systematic process of rigorously discussing "how?" questioning, tenaciously following through, and ensuring accountability. It includes linking the organization's mission, vision, and strategy to implementation, creating an action-oriented culture of accountability, connecting the strategy to operations, and robust communication. When leaders execute effectively, they get smart answers to their questions.

How Efficiency Changes the Game certainly explains the links between efficiency and productivity, but it does more. It clarifies what the game needs to be and how leaders can use their influence to disrupt that status quo to create all new games, ones of their own creation and ones for which they have set the rules. Disruptive Leaders™ see disruption as positive and mandatory, and they understand that if they don't cause the disruption, someone else will.

Joseph Schumpeter, one of the most influential economists of the early 20th century, popularized the term "creative destruction" to warn against the repetitive process of recycling the old into new. According to him, the economy is a living organism that constantly grows and adapts to changes. Over the years, Schumpeter has garnered much attention and worldwide approval and has helped mankind advance through the economic world. We should now think of Ray Hodge as Schumpeter's modern-day disciple—the person who will help us understand what we must do to emerge from the global pandemic.

Creative destruction involves the dismantling of long-standing practices to make way for innovation. Schumpeter originally advocated creative destruction in manufacturing processes that increase productivity and described creative destruction as the "process of industrial mutation that incessantly revolutionizes the economic structure from within, incessantly destroying the old one, incessantly creating a new one." Recently we have started to use the term in other industries, especially those that rely heavily on technology.

Creative destruction describes the *deliberate* dismantling of established processes that make way for improved methods of production. Ray takes Schumpeter's ideas a step further to offer key insights:

- Rest is the fertile soil from which quality work springs.
- We tend to look at the past to learn from mistakes, but too few leaders deconstruct their success, much less celebrate them. Intentionally reflecting allows a clearer view of the past and a more optimistic vision of the future.
- Planning keeps us from running in circles, constantly focusing on *inputs* rather than *results*.
- Delegating both tasks and decisions to the most junior person in the organization, *along with the authority to carry them out,* allows everyone to use time more efficiently and effectively.

Of course, none of this can happen without a culture of trust. Employees must trust their leaders to make the right decisions, to behave ethically, and to care about them. Leaders, in turn, must trust those in their chains-of-command to commit to, not merely comply with, excellence standards.

Successful companies with established products *will* get pushed aside as the world recovers, unless their leaders know how and when to abandon traditional business practices and welcome change. Ray Hodge has written the roadmap about how to do that. His sage advice and in-the-trenches experience equip him to shine the light into the future to help companies recover from setbacks the global pandemic has created and to position themselves for more growth and prosperity in any economy of the future.

Linda Henman, PhD
Author of *Risky Business: Why You Must Develop a Disruptive Mindset*, among other works

Acknowledgments

Books reflect the journeys of their authors and, along those pathways, there are often important people who direct, guide, and help in the process. This book represents part of my journey in leadership and consulting that has involved significant others for whom I am incredibly grateful.

My previous business partner from many years ago, Brook Monahan, who originally provided a powerful model of efficient working, taught me the importance of focus. My long-term mentor and sometimes personal coach, Dr. Alan Weiss has been instrumental in shaping my work and particularly for encouraging me to make my own efficiency work more efficient which he termed *lean on lean*. I have also been blessed to be part of Alan's global community of consultants of which I am grateful for their insights and suggestions as to implementing best practices along the way. Colin Noyes, a long-term friend and advisor on leadership coaching, has provided countless insights into the nature of people and how to bring the best out of them. Another long-term friend, Dr. Robert Floyd has had a significant part to play in being a sounding board for many of the embryonic concepts and deliberations, helping me form, develop, and consolidate these into my thinking and practices. For Shawn Butterfield and the thought-provoking discussions around Duck Hunters and Snipers, and the many other concepts we have discussed, and for the hundreds of business owners and executives, I have met with and worked with over the years I am truly grateful, with many now considered as friends.

And for those who have been involved in the writing of this book. My current business advisor, Dr. Linda Henman helped me formulate the concept and outline along with the *Foreword* she has written. For B.T. and the wonderful team at the Warradale Hotel who have cheerfully served me (and not kicked me out for overstaying) as I worked on the manuscript. For Clifton Warren who took valuable time to review this work and provide feedback and for the team at Business Expert Press who have made this book possible. And finally for my partner Michelle. Her ability to cope with my absences in the writing of this book along with her encouragement, support, and directing me in the process has been amazing.

Introduction

Efficiency as a practice for me has developed over the years and was informed by my own personal and organizational challenges. This was necessary because, in the early days of being in business, I made the mistake of compensating for my inefficiencies by applying more hours. But I came to see the issue wasn't my business, it was me. Gradually I discovered straightforward routes rather than the lengthy, well-trod circuitous ones I had been taking.

Throughout a 10-year period of operating a finance business, I became increasingly bored with writing home loan applications, which led me to the discovery that my enjoyment was in the consulting, creative thinking, and strategic side of the business: working with those who were facing complex situations for getting ahead financially. From this *enjoyment discovery*, I decided to move into consulting full time. It was the winter of 2010 when I met with the directors of a company who would become one of my first clients. In that initial meeting, they told me they did not want to increase their sales or profitability but rather they needed assistance to bring *order out of their chaos*. Those words powerfully connected to my own efficiency journey from the previous decade and powerfully launched my new career.

In my consulting work, I have become accustomed to discovering concealed waste in every corner of a business. From people who have been placed in the wrong role and simply work in inefficient ways to duplications, errors, and technology issues within workflows, and that is just the start. Inefficiencies render leaders and organizations vulnerable to failure. At a business level, these inefficiencies contribute toward a *noncompetitive* advantage, negatively impacting such areas as financial performance, quality, delivery times, employee and customer satisfaction levels, agility, and future growth. And at a personal level, the effect on leaders results in working onerous hours, sleep difficulties, significant stress levels, relationship challenges, poor health, and no time for *play*.

This book offers efficient applications that can be immediately applied and are derived from my in-the-field learning while supported in places by research and actual examples. Given that some supply products and others provide services, I have chosen to use the word *products* to combine the two. Throughout this book, I reference many of the organizations and people I have worked with and, while remaining true to the actual events, I have disguised many of the situations to provide for confidentiality.

And finally, at the time of this writing, the world is in the grip of the COVID-19 pandemic. While lean operations and holding a strong competitive advantage are important in the best of times, the current economic climate makes it critical that our organizations are as efficient, lean, and nimble as is their potential.

CHAPTER 1

Leadership

Mirror, Mirror on the Wall…

Game Changer: *Efficiency does not happen of its own accord but is driven into every corner of a business through leaders dedicated to optimizing their operations. The quality of our leadership is mirrored in the health and well-being of our organizations.*

In a large city, two businesses were providing similar products to a similar market that existed in neighboring suburbs. One business was owned by a man who always complained about his staff. They turned up late, stole goods from him and he was always having to hire new people to keep up with the outflow of his *bad employees*. He struggled to make money and his store was anything but tidy. Inefficiency reigned supreme. The other business was incredibly efficient. It was operated by a woman who spoke highly of her people and in turn, they spoke highly of her. There was no staff turnover to speak of, the place was clean and tidy, there were systems in place, and the business was profitable. The outcomes in both these businesses fully reflected their leaders.

If we look at ourselves in a glass mirror, the reflection is precisely what we look like at the time. And business is similar: reflecting in all the various functions and outcomes, its leadership. This reflection tells you who you are as a leader, serving to instruct and guide you. Sometimes we receive great personal encouragement from this reflection, affirming us in the decisions we have made and the actions we have taken. At other times, we see outcomes that are less than desired, indicating changes are required in our own leadership abilities or the need for broader organizational corrections. Whatever the mirror reveals, it points back to leadership.

The Efficient Leader

Four Foundational Leadership Disciplines That Drive Efficiency

While many disciplines could be covered here, I have chosen four of the most common ones that, from my observations, significantly impact organizational efficiencies.

1. Rest

Rest is the fertile soil from which quality work springs from.

Rest is often relegated to that of a secondary activity—that which we have to do in order to work more tomorrow. Many of us have grown up in an environment where the emphasis was placed on working hard and working long, and, if we did this, we stood a better chance of being successful. Productivity was driven from more hours at the office with success attributed to financial gains and security through effort. Work thus became the centrality of focus for one's life with all other aspects taking a distant second, including rest.

Rest provides the context for clear thinking. A cluttered, racing mind outputs fragmented directives and diluted efforts, where multitasking becomes the norm, things are never fully completed, and people feel neglected. Efficiency is no friend to the disorganized mind but for the one where the discipline of rest is seen as an equal partner to their work, clarity of thought with cohesive actions will impact organizational efficiencies, and often, with an ease and flow we are unaware of.

Early in my business career, I thought that working long hours would create success fast. I would often turn up to the office on Wednesday morning having worked 36 hours in the previous two days. While there is no substitute for *focused* effort, relegating sleep to a few hours a night caught up with me. I would walk the edges of burnout every six months or so, losing weeks of momentum as I recovered. It was a case of learning the hard way. I eventually started seeing a naturopath who highlighted the need to stop living on adrenaline and start living out of rest, the foundation of which was a good night's sleep. Instead of viewing sleep as unproductive time, I came to understand it was the perfect partner of productivity. They were two sides of the same coin.

Sleep deficit impacts workplaces in significant ways. A study conducted on four corporations in the United States found that safety, productivity, and performance were significantly worse for those employees who suffered from insomnia and insufficient sleep, concluding that "Sleep disturbances contribute to decreased employee productivity at a high cost to employers."[1]

Dr. Michael A. Grandner, Director of the Sleep and Health Research Program at the University of Arizona, says:

> Workplace health initiatives should promote the idea that sleep is not unproductive time. Rather, it is an investment of time that has been shown to produce improved productivity and less productivity loss. The available evidence shows that rather than more productive, individuals who are sleeping less are actually less productive, even with more time. The culture of sleep being only "rest" and therefore a sign of weakness or lack of endurance needs to change. (Grandner 2018; p. 1631)

One major contributing factor to poor sleep is the inability to psychologically detach from our work. Numerous leaders have mentioned how they wake during the night with their minds racing, with many of their partners saying they are physically present but emotionally absent when they are home. One process I have found extremely beneficial to assist the detachment process is what I have called *closing the door on the day.* Fifteen to 30 minutes before leaving the office, review your day's accomplishments, and then create your plan for the following day, ensuring all your *yet to be done* tasks have been scheduled. Then, intentionally put your computer to sleep and, as you walk out, purposefully close the door.

One of the other issues that contribute to our struggle to detach from work is a racing mind, filled with uncompleted tasks. A highly effective method is simply getting them out of the mind by writing them onto a page, purposefully allocating them to be actioned tomorrow. If and when they reappear in our minds we can tell ourselves that "yes, I have written that down and it will be dealt with tomorrow," assuring the mind we have it under control. When we have closed the door on the day and have settled our minds, a good night's rest is made easier.

Rest is also about *deliberately* taking breaks, to calm the mind and relax the body. Rest is an activity that does not demand of us nor does it automatically insert itself in our diaries. We have to be intentional in creating space for it. Asking a business owner what personal goals she would like to achieve in the coming year, she mentioned one was to have a daily nap and the other to have Friday afternoons off. When I asked why they couldn't enact it immediately they said it was guilt driven: if their employees had to work full days then so should they. Leaders often think they have to arrive at work first and depart last so they are seen to be leading by example. But to take time out for daily rest and regular play not only is personally rewarding, but also models the importance of rest to our people. Because busyness is often erroneously equated with productivity, we view downtime as wasted time, thus increasing the feelings of guilt, but as Alex Soojung-Kim Pang, author of the book *Rest*, emphasizes: "Too often busyness is not a means to accomplishment but an obstacle to it. Deliberate rest helps you recognize and avoid the trap of pointless busyness and concentrate instead on what's important."[2]

2. Reflection

Working from a rested position with a calm mind helps us in the process of reflection. The word reflection, from its Latin origin, means *bent back*[3] with one definition being "the return of light or sound waves from a surface."[4] While we view the *effects* of our leadership being *bent back* through the business mirror, it then becomes important to stop and personally reflect on the *why*. Why has this happened? Why did we gain such success here? Why are customer complaints increasing? Why is the team so happy of late? Pausing from doing the work, long enough to reflect on the impact of our work: deconstructing our successes, thinking through our challenges, and failures, enables greater effectiveness in the present with faster and more precise and efficient movement forward.

Some time ago I saw in the mirror of my business a plummeting conversion ratio from proposals to sales. My immediate reaction was to work harder at increasing my proposal output but instead I paused, reflected on what I was seeing, and as a result gained significant insight into the reason for the decline. I was neglecting to fulfill some of the critical aspects of the proposal/sale process that had proven themselves when my ratios were higher. From my review, reflection, and making the subsequent changes, my ratios went from 25 percent to 72 percent within the following few months. This wouldn't have happened had I not paused to reflect, seeking to gain distinctive insights to move forward.

One of the advantages of reflection is that we can learn from our *yesterdays* to perform more effectively in our *tomorrows*. Musician Pat Metheny demonstrates this. He has kept a postshow diary for the thousands of performances he has played and among the many insights the diaries provide he says, "It sounds weird, but over time the journal has helped me work out that I shouldn't eat before a show. I play better when I'm hungry."[5] How would anyone detect that eating affects one's playing if they hadn't exercised the discipline of reflection? And it's often the undetected performance nuances that go unnoticed in the rush of leadership busyness that locks us into *playing as we have always played* instead of increasing the effectiveness of our work.

3. Planning

While I cover this subject in detail in Chapter 3, it is important to mention planning here as it is a fundamental discipline of effective leadership. Planning reduces anxiety and the temptation to be reactive. It enables the leader to take a more considered approach with less energy expended on secondary issues. Planning is central to efficiency and the accomplishment of strategic objectives, enabling us to be methodical in our work and build something of worth. What construction company begins a building project without first drawing up the plans? What war general goes into battle without having first strategically planned the process? What sports coach goes into a game without a plan to beat the competition and win the contest? Yet, for many in leadership, they don't approach their work and their days with a planned approach but rather default to a more reactive style of task and people management. Thorough planning lays the groundwork from which efficient and meaningful activity ensues.

4. Delegation

Speaking with a senior manager recently, he mentioned he performed most of the requests that came his way. Despite having a team of responsible people around him he experienced guilt when he thought of delegating tasks to others. One business owner I was working with struggled to delegate due to their need to feel important. Being overloaded fuelled their sense of self-worth. Many other leaders I have coached have reverted to doing tasks themselves for the sake of speed and quality: they want it done well, they want it done now, so they perform it solo. And yet other managers fear if they are too proficient in delegation, they may effectively make themselves redundant, thus placing their jobs at risk.

Chapter 3 will cover the practical aspects of how to delegate effectively but for our purposes here, consider the following positive benefits delegation can have.

- It enables leaders to expand their role capacities and work scope.
- When others are entrusted with tasks, it often contributes to their sense of value to the organization.
- It optimizes individual strengths.
- It promotes growth within the individual, especially when it is combined with specific improvement training.
- Focus on high-priority items can be maintained while secondary tasks are being fulfilled by others.
- The concept of team is promoted more effectively.
- It's efficient.

Richard Branson notes: "it's a fairy tale to think that you can do everything by yourself." He goes on to say, "It's vital to the success of your business that you learn to hand off those things that you aren't able to do well."[6] And I think Richard is someone worth emulating in this regard.

Three Habits That Undermine Efficiency

1. Erratic Work Styles

Efficiency is undermined by erratic leadership. If leadership's management style is largely one of reactivity—an erratic style where leaders display a continuous, almost involuntary, and spontaneous reaction to issues, tasks, and requests with the absence of forethought, planning, and strategic execution—efficiency is effectively stinted.

One of the companies I consulted within the health industry was in a significant growth phase. Their primary challenge was in managing the existing workloads and people while continuing to absorb the current expansion opportunities. The business owner was best described as spontaneous and erratic. They had grown several companies from the ground up, were exceptional at it, and asked me to work with their management team to ensure the business continued to expand without imploding. While they saw the need for managing growth their erratic work style continually undermined any structure and progress we were bringing to the management foundations. I took them aside partway through the project and told them that the biggest cause of the ongoing unrest, unhappiness, and constant chaos in the business was them. From that discussion, they chose not to change, rarely communicated with me, and continued to throw daily grenades into the business. The business mirrored their style perfectly.

One of the traits smart leaders exhibit is the recognition of who they are and who they aren't. Smart leaders have the wisdom to understand those weaknesses that are contributing to inefficiency and lack of organizational performance and seek to shore those weaknesses up through education and coaching. They also employ others with complementary strengths, having the wisdom to let those complementary partners run their race and trusting them in the process.

2. Circle Running

One of the outcomes of the reactive and erratic management style is that of *circle running*. "I feel like I've been running in circles" is the oft-heard statement. Moving at lightning speed, bouncing this way and that, we kick up a lot of dust but don't progress too far. No matter how far along the leadership track we are, most, if not all, certainly experience this from time to time. However, to have this as a lifelong work pattern only gets us running the same circuitous route. I have met business owners in their late 50s and early 60s who have confessed they have operated in this style for many years and with the prospect of retirement on the horizon, they've realized unless they change by creating strategic objectives they can align their daily actions to, the postwork years are likely to be difficult.

Removing ourselves from circle running and learning a new way of operating (especially if it has been our work style for many years) is a courageous act for many. I've seen leaders achieve this shift but it happened with initial insight that there is a better way, educating themselves in time management and delegation along with the integration of leadership coaching and ongoing accountability. And when they revert to previous behaviors (which they always do in the early stages), they realize it is part of the learning process. Circle running limits forward movement and promotes inefficiencies. The straighter the line we can run, the more effective we are as leaders.

3. Lack of Trust

The owners of a nutritional supplements company had placed their trust in one of their divisional managers for many years. He was like a son to them and then the unthinkable happened. They discovered he had been ordering supplies for various customers and was selling a portion of them for his own personal gain. Trust can be destroyed in an instant.

Benjamin Kutsyuruba and Keith D. Walker write:

It is well known that trust is an essential, yet a fragile part of organizational life. Because trust sometimes has to be placed without guarantees, it will inevitably be broken, violated, and damaged when parties involved in trustworthy relationships let others down. When trust-destroying events occur, trust is shattered and its level plummets quickly into the domain of distrust. (Walker and Kutsyuruba 2016)

Trust involves risk but, without taking that risk, leadership quickly becomes the bottleneck through doing too much themselves. This along with the micromanagement of our people tells employees they are there to do what they're told, stifling creativity and initiative. When trust has been broken, instead of setting up checks and balances to mitigate further risk and continue to trust (which the aforementioned business owners did), the prevalent tendency is to regain control, take back the reins, and do more ourselves. This effectively starts a process where we as leaders become contained within our own worlds, where we don't trust and we fail to listen. Leaders, in taking back the reins, often default to a more authoritarian style and while this approach has its place in certain situations, its effect on broader efficiencies can be detrimental.

Believing in others communicates value and when you combine trust along with an open approach to listening and learning, from the storeman through to senior management, efficiency gains can be rapid.

The Efficient Management Team

Operating on a United Front

Divided management teams create divided organizations: person against person, department against department, fighting over resources with each attempting to get their own way. Divided management teams are reflected in the broader organization with their attitudes and actions cascading down, affecting all those in their wake. And rather than a central strategic agenda running through the core that galvanizes efforts and a team agenda, managers with their own agendas create more havoc than they do good. And this aids in creating greater inefficiencies. Rather than a cohesive flow between people and systems, there becomes a disconnectedness throughout.

When a military squad is assigned a mission, to accomplish its goal each has to focus on the same target while watching and protecting each other's backs. Individually they may have different thoughts of how to achieve the mission but unity is crucial for success. Team sports are similar. The goal is to win every game and while there are strengths and weaknesses within the group, playing *as a team* increases the chances of success. And management teams are no different.

Respect and Connection

At the heart of unity is respect. Managers don't necessarily need to be friends, nor do they have to like everyone on the team but they do need to show respect for each other along with having the capacity to support each other when required. Some of the best management teams I have worked with have been those where individuals enjoyed being with each other, and this is often a reflection of the senior leader. While the managers might say they'd never do anything personally with the others outside of work, they had connection and demonstrated respect for each other in the workplace. They honored each other's strengths and covered their weaknesses. And while their meetings always involve operational and performance issues, there is often laughter and genuine enjoyment about being in the same room with each other. The senior leader in these cases often promotes out-of-work discussion, demonstrating interest in the personal lives of those they lead. These more personable leaders have a way of connecting their management teams at more a human level, with the interconnectivity increasing the team's engagement thus their corresponding productivity. I have also observed that meetings over food and after-hours social occasions go a long way in promoting this cohesive management front.

Value Systems

Each of your managers has their own value system, and values represent the prioritization of what we prefer in life. And each organization has its own value system, whether this is documented or not. Where this comes unstuck is when different people express different values to that of the corporate values. As an organization, we might value high customer and staff satisfaction where we treat everyone with respect. That works well for most except for, hypothetically, the sales manager who is disrespectful to the customers he deals with. While most of the managers share this corporate value, the sales manager persistently demonstrates a behavior, stemming from his value system that is at odds with the whole. To gain a coordinated front, the senior leader, along with other managers, must address these kinds of behaviors candidly. Sometimes, the proverbial slap in the head along with starting a regular counseling process to help the manager both see and demonstrate a value shift can be the improvement process in and of itself. But sometimes it means either repositioning the person (as in the case of the sales manager repositioned away from customer-interfacing roles) or helping them depart the organization. When these situations are not actively dealt with, the emotional angst of our personnel increases which in turn affects efficiencies. One of the ways you know this emotional angst temperature is on the rise is by how much time is spent thinking about the issue, talking to others about it, and time spent dealing with the actual person. I have often pointed out to leaders I am coaching that we are spending far too much time talking about the person and that fast, decisive action is required to prevent further negativity infecting the team and the resulting performance loss.

Given each person has a different value system and the organization also has its value system, senior leadership needs to consistently hold the corporate values banner high, always seeking to ensure the team is *aligned in mind* and behaviors.

Weeding

After the first day of consulting with a company, I commented to the business owner it was one of the best teams I had ever observed. "We've done lots of weeding," he responded, and sometimes, there are people on our teams that aren't quite the right fit. Jim Collins, in his explanation about the findings from research conducted for his book *Good to Great*, writes:

> When we began the research project, we expected to find that the first step in taking a company from good to great would be to set a new direction, a new vision and strategy for the company, and then to get people committed and aligned behind that new direction. We found something quite the opposite.
>
> The executive who ignited the transformations from good to great did not first figure out where to drive the bus and then get people to take it there. No, they *first* got the right people on the bus (and the wrong people off the bus) and *then* figured out where to drive it. (Collins 2001; p. 41)

Those we deem to be the wrong people on the bus may be highly skilled, but if they are solo players and disrespectful to others, weeding is often the best option. I have seen companies flourish quickly after the wrong managers were helped to exit.

Strategic Alignment

A compelling vision as part of the strategic directive marshalls the energies of an organization and by its very nature drives efficiencies toward its fulfillment. While I cover the topic of strategy in Chapter 2, it is important to note here that organizations that have strong strategic objectives, that have a collective commitment by management to their overriding mission, and where a *strong reason for being* exists increase their chances significantly of creating a team that is unified in terms of purpose.

When different managers operate from unchecked personal values that drive unchecked individual behaviors and all with different goals, fragmentation, not unity, is the effect. It is important to ensure that senior leadership is regularly revisiting who they are and what they stand for (their values), along with the strategic objectives. When all managers express the same values and are focused on the same goals, efficiency gains velocity. A unified management team is truly a game changer.

Reflection Point

- In reflecting on the subject of leadership, where do you see your personal strengths and weaknesses are?
- Where do you see that your organization could do better in terms of its leadership?
- What are you seeing reflected in the mirror of your organization?

Summary

Changing the efficiency game starts at the top, with leadership. It is important for leaders to:

- Operate from a place of rest and reflect more on their work and the effectiveness of their organization or the department they are responsible for.
- Plan their days and be highly effective in delegation.
- Demonstrate a teachable attitude with a lifelong pursuit of personal development and increasing skill set effectiveness.

- Be personable in their dealings with others.
- Work toward the unity of their colleagues and always have each other's backs.
- Trust others while maintaining effective checks and balances.
- Ensure all team members are contributing to the strategic direction and anyone who is not is helped to get onboard or exit the bus.

Effective leaders are those who when they look out across their organization will see an image reflected back they can increasingly be proud of. The game being played in front of their eyes will show them what they are doing well and what to correct, thus continually driving efficiencies into all aspects of their business.

Endnotes

1. (Rosekind et al. 2010; p. 91).
2. (Pang 2018; p. 242).
3. (Harper 2001–2020).
4. (Merriam-Webster, Incorporated 1828–2020).
5. (Baily 2020).
6. (Clarkson 2015).

CHAPTER 2

Strategy

Go Direct—Go with Speed

Game Changer: *If you don't know where you are going or map the direct route, you're destined for a long trip. But when we establish a destination, map the path, and execute specific actions, rapid momentum ensues.*

When my children were young, we would sometimes pile them in the car, head out from home with no destination in mind. Arriving at an intersection I would ask, "Should we go right, left, or straight ahead?" As we would drive to "destination unknown" the invariable question (and often irritatingly repeated) would be asked, "Are we there yet?" While the road trip started with fun and energy, they would quickly grow weary on the way to nowhere.

Organizations are not too dissimilar, often traveling the roads to *destination nowhere.* Having an endpoint is critical for without a clearly defined future and aligned actions, we too easily become inefficient and wayward. A lean operation is derived from knowing where we are going and taking the most direct route to get there. Having a clearly defined strategy that represents our future state drives efficiencies throughout the organization. Containing a central compelling vision and achievable objectives that planning is connected to, every activity can be placed under the strategic microscope to ascertain whether it contributes to and is in alignment with our future, or should be deemed as waste. Thus our strategy becomes the directive by which all decisions are weighed against. The time taken in strategy work is often paid back multifold due to the speed at which decisions can be made. One of your managers has a great idea about an extra market to chase. Under the strategy light, you see very quickly this is a red herring and the importance of maintaining focus on building current momentum within the markets you have previously committed to. This is one of many examples where, instead of leadership deliberating for weeks, trialing the new market, and finding out it was a waste of time and resources, having a clearly defined strategy and measuring all current results and future activities against can be a game changer. Each of you reading this will more than likely fit into one of three categories:

1. You believe that strategy and planning are important but are weak on tactical execution.
2. You believe that only action counts. As long as you have some future idea in mind and you keep up the momentum, that is all that matters.
3. You believe that all action needs to be directed and measured against a strategic framework and is critical for success. You adhere to this regularly.

What Is Strategy?

People use the word strategy in many different contexts: husband/wife finding strategies, body-building strategies, friend avoidance strategies, cleaning strategies, and so on. When it comes to business, there are marketing strategies, pricing strategies, sales strategies, and HR strategies. As I listen to the use of the term across these various contexts I often wonder what strategy means. Does it mean a way of achieving goals, planning, tactics, direction, goals, methodology? It's often hard to tell.

The word strategy had its origins in war. As researcher Willie Pietersen notes,

> Yet for much of modern history the word "strategy" seldom appeared in the business vernacular. The concept, derived from the Greek *strategia*—a compound of *stratos,* meaning "army," and *agein,* meaning "to lead"—was instead born in the military. (Pietersen 2016)

If we looked at strategy from a military viewpoint, the focus would be on gaining the advantage over an enemy and seeking to defeat them.

From its origin, we can see why the term *competitive advantage* has its roots in history and is linked to strategy. Much of the organizational strategic work that takes place in today's world is focused on gaining an advantage over our competition. While this is relevant in a crowded market place where there are only a defined amount of buyers and sellers, strategic work is also related to creating new buyers in new markets and creating opportunities where others have failed to see it.

Strategy is about *endpoints,* connecting where we are today with an ideal future state, effectively a top-down process. Expert organizational strategists would suggest that strategy is:

"the framework which guides those choices that determine the nature and direction of an organization."[1]

"a coherent set of analyses, concepts, policies, arguments and actions that respond to a high-stakes challenge."[2]

"a collection of insights that compellingly explain why you do what you do, and for whom, and that provides a framework for decisions to be made."[3]

"a process by which significant decisions that establish the nature and direction of the organization are made and which establishes the policies and beliefs that will help the organization to achieve those ends."[4]

From these statements, we can define strategy as:

- Directional.
- Cohesive in all respects.
- Purpose driven.
- Achievement oriented.
- Focused and concise.
- A framework for decision making.

You will notice none of these experts mention planning. The mistake many organizations make in strategy formulation is they start from the bottom up, using current data in the various areas of their business and then forecasting growth over a certain time frame. These forecasts tend to be nothing more than arbitrary hopes, based on what they *think* they can achieve, and often lack tactical firepower behind them, not adequately addressing strategic direction. Strategy is not planning, thus the term strategic planning is somewhat misleading. Strategy is the *what*, planning is the *how*. Thus, planning takes its place once the strategic direction has been established. Planning done too early in the process effectively aborts the strategic process.[5]

The Strategic Framework

Within the strategic framework, as seen in Figure 2.1, there are nine fundamental areas to consider.

1. Vision. What does our ideal future look like?
2. Purpose. Why are we here?
3. Values. What principles will we stand for?
4. Critical Objectives. What are those objectives that are critical to our strategic achievement?

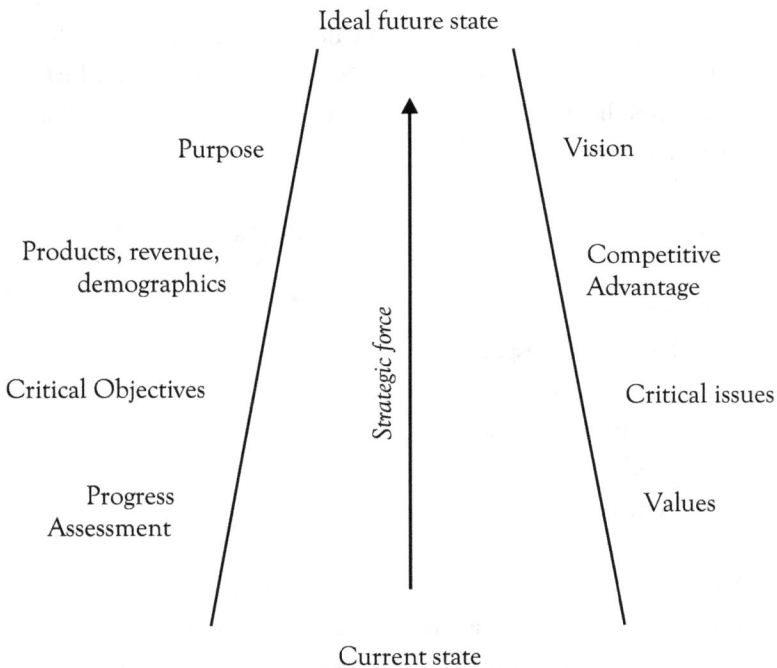

Ideal future state

Purpose

Vision

Products, revenue, demographics

Competitive Advantage

Strategic force

Critical Objectives

Critical issues

Progress Assessment

Values

Current state

Figure 2.1 The strategic framework

5. Critical Issues. What are the major areas that could present as obstacles to achieving our objectives?
6. Progress Assessment. What milestones and metrics will we use to assess progress and who will keep us accountable to these?
7. Competitive Advantage. What makes us unique and distinct that will drive our competitive advantage in the market place and by which we will be known?
8. Products, Revenues, and Demographics. What do we provide and what could we provide? What revenues are ideal from these products and to which demographics should we be focused on?
9. Strategic Force. What will be our enabler or leverage tool that will empower our forward progress toward our ideal future state?

1. Vision

An articulated vision that is compelling and achievable sets the pathway toward the future strategic state. John F. Kennedy's *man on the moon vision* is perhaps one of the most powerful examples of a compelling vision. He believed America "should commit itself to achieving the goal, before this decade is out, of landing a man on the moon and returning him safely to the earth."[6] In a subsequent speech at Rice University's Rice Stadium, Kennedy declared:

> We choose to go to the moon. We choose to go to the moon in this decade ... because that goal will serve to organize and measure the best of our energies and skills, because that challenge is one that we are willing to accept, one we are unwilling to postpone, and one which we intend to win ... (Kennedy 1962)

A vision that compels. A vision with a time frame. A vision that is said to *organize and measure the best of our energies and skills.* Forbes senior contributor Carmine Gallo said,

> At the time Kennedy presented his vision few scientists thought a moon landing could be accomplished, especially in less than ten years. Thousands of details had not been figured out. Rockets had

not been designed, computers were not up to the task and nobody quite knew how to keep astronauts alive in space. But big, bold visions have a way of inspiring teams. The goal itself was intoxicating and had the effect of changing the conversation. Scientists who had said, "It can't be done," instead began saying, "Well, it's going to be hard, but if we were to do it by the end of the decade, how would we do it?" (Gallo 2011)

Vision is about *seeing*, and compelling vision statements enable hearers *to see*. Think of Microsoft's original vision: a *computer on every desk in every home*. Another visual declaration. If Bill Gates had said that Microsoft would be the *leader in computer sales*, I suspect that more than a few would have started yawning at the point.

Both landing a man on the moon and a computer on every desk create powerful pictures in our minds. And these visionary pictures, when conveyed and *lived* by effective leaders throughout an organization, morph into the beliefs and actions of its people. Vision helps create our ideal future state which harnesses energies and resources to efficiently drive toward that destination. And in the case of landing a man on the moon and a computer on every desk, these very vision statements created a competitive advantage for both America and Microsoft.

Reflection Point

- What is your vision?
- Does it energize you?
- Will the achievement of your vision provide you with a competitive advantage?

2. Purpose

Purpose is all about the *why*, our reason for existence. When a sense of purpose pervades an organization, it provides its people with a greater reason for being, connecting their daily work to more meaningful and deeper intentions. Clarifying purpose can also provide us with a competitive advantage over others and these are often stated as an organization's tagline. One residential builder might say their purpose is *providing quality homes at affordable prices* whereas another builder offering similar designs to a similar demographic might lead with the statement, *where families play together.* The first tagline is general, with the second purposeful, connecting the business with the ideal buyer underpinned with purpose, providing them with a significant edge in the marketplace when selling homes to families. Purpose is a powerful conduit between our people and our customers. When employees *see* our vision and capture a sense of *ownership* around the purpose that drives us toward that vision, it creates a powerful underlying force.

Reflection Point

- What is your organization's purpose?
- Does your tagline connect with your purpose?

3. Values

Values represent the priority of our preferences and are the principles we stand by and want to be known by. These principles become the non-negotiables, providing a bedrock for corporate behavior—both internally and externally, along with shaping our cultures.

A recent story relating to the coffee chain XS Espresso mentioned a barista at one of their local stores was stood down from his job by his manager because of his skin color. The manager's reason for the dismissal was that the local patrons preferred the other in-house barista because he was white. The company responded publicly by saying, "As a brand we stand in solidarity against systemic racism, and are extremely disheartened and grieved that inequality was amongst us. As a company we are auditing every part of our business to uncover racism and inequality."[7]

This story represents the centrality of values and how they govern behavior and efficient decision making. Instead of deliberating for days, decisive action can be taken immediately, thus continuing to drive us toward our ideal future state with minimal disruption. Value behavioral conflicts will always happen (given there are human beings involved that don't always share the corporate values) but a business that holds up the banner of their immovable principles and seeks to integrate these through constant reinforcement and active education will be an organization that attract others with similar ideals. Strategy is about our ideal future and values represent who we want to be and stand for in the marketplace, to our stakeholders, staff, and customers.

Reflection Point

- What are the values your organization stands by?

4. Critical Objectives

When I was body-building, my trainer helped me establish an endpoint: what I would weigh, how much fat my body would have, my cardio level, and so on. These represented my future self or, in our strategic terms here, the ideal future state. My trainer then deconstructed this longer term *ideal* into shorter term objectives that I would, with singular focus and concentration, work toward. If I didn't have shorter term objectives to focus on, my training would have been wayward. I would have shown up at the gym and wandered from machine to machine without any singularity of focus for the achievement of the next-stage objective. The ideal future self was too *out there* to achieve any real progress in the shorter term. Having achievable objectives that were in line with the ideal future self, focused all of my immediate attention on these. Strategy expert Richard Rumelt in his book *Good Strategy Bad Strategy* says,

> One of the leader's most powerful tools is the creation of a good proximate objective—one that is close enough at hand to be feasible. A proximate objective names a target that the organization can reasonably be expected to hit, even overwhelm. (Rumelt 2017)

Critical or proximate objectives are decisive points. Like steps on a ladder, we know the next move to make in the direction of our ideal future state while enabling the concentration of focus, energy, and resources toward their fulfillment.

5. Critical Issues

Critical issues are those obstacles (either current or perceived) that have a high likelihood of impacting the achievement of the predefined objectives. When we set objectives without identifying issues that could potentially hinder or block our advancement, resources can be squandered through an inadequate identification process.

Reflection Point

- In Table 2.1, list three critical objectives, the related potential critical issues, and why they are important to address in the achievement of your objectives.

Table 2.1 Critical issues

Critical objective	Critical issue	Why is this important?

6. Progress Assessment

In the days when I was learning ballroom dancing, I was on a pathway to perform in competitions, *my ideal future state*. At various intervals, I would be assigned to the senior teacher where she would test me on all the previous stage's sequences to assess whether I was ready to progress to the next level. It was not a random approach but a structured path with assessments along the way. Similarly, when designing our strategic future along with the critical objectives, both regular assessment intervals and defining the metrics to use in assessing progress are essential for detecting and correcting deviations. In the case of my dancing, when assessments were made, if there were sequences or style issues I hadn't quite mastered, the timing for next-level focus would be delayed while they were being corrected.

If, for example, part of our ideal future within the next five years is to generate sales from each state within our country and there are five we haven't impacted yet, one critical objective might be to establish our presence in one state per annum. But how will we assess progress? Will it mean a physical office in each state? A certain percentage of group revenue from each state or a 10-person salesforce trained and selling an average of $400,000 of product each per month? The more detailed we are with defining how progress will be assessed will be one of the determinates of the success or failure of meeting those objectives.

Reflection Point

- In Table 2.2, outline the metrics you will use to assess progress toward three of your critical objectives.

Table 2.2 Critical objectives with metrics

Critical objective	Metrics to assess progress

7. Competitive Advantage

In today's world of similar businesses serving similar sectors, industries, and customer demographics, being able to identify the edge we currently have or design the edge that will cause us to stand out in the crowd while providing high value to the customer is critical in the strategic process and the longevity of our organizations. And this is particularly relevant when events like the global pandemic impact the survival of businesses to the scale it has.

The words *competitive advantage* indicate the ability of an organization to gain an advantage over its competitors. And the basis for winning any competition is having the smarts and skill set to give you the upper hand to win, along with a depth of intelligent insight into the opposition's game plan.

Competitor Analysis

When working to define your competitive advantage, understanding what the competition is doing is fundamental to the process.

When I first started my mortgage broking business back in 2001, I soon realized that every second person I met (especially at networking events) was another mortgage broker and were all advertising the same thing: We come to you; 30 banks to choose from; fast approvals; cheapest interest rates; and so on. This was further validated when I conducted competitor research by reviewing many of my competitor's advertisements in numerous magazines. It was then I noticed a major opening in the market. Rarely was any broker promoting their services to multiple property owners—the investors—but rather, the majority were fixated on first and general homeowners. I then pivoted the focus of my entire business on this one thing. It was an early lesson in gaining advantage through competitor analysis and provided me with significant external distinction in a very crowded marketplace.

In conducting analysis I would suggest researching the following areas of your competitors:

- Physical location and the geographical reach of their business.
- What they are communicating in their mission, vision, and value statements.
- Quality and brand reinforcement through suppliers and partnerships.
- Credibility through testimonials, guarantees, recognized client logos and names, awards.
- Products they provide.
- Any feature product they promote.
- Pricing models.
- What is the benefit they are selling?
- Primary target market.
- Secondary target market.
- The mediums they are promoting their business through, for example, social media, radio, newspapers.

- What is their core promotional pitch?
- What is projected in terms of reputation and image?
- What is their point of difference and how do they communicate it?
- Other pertinent information.

Reflection Point

- When you consider your competitors, how can you position yourself more effectively?

Internal Strengths and Weaknesses

Internal strengths relate to what we excel at as an organization. This is not done in comparison to others but simply identifying the major strengths we operate within. Some of those clients I've worked with have identified theirs as customer relationships; their sales force; purpose-built job management systems or the underlying strength of their technology; the design team; marketing know-how; speed; systemization; reverse engineering to arrive at complex solutions; their people; a comprehensive provider of all solutions required by the customer. As a mortgage broker, my unique strength was creativity and now as a consultant, one of my primary strengths is the speed of insight into the root cause of inefficiencies whether it be process or people related. Our internal strengths are unique to us and even if your competitors demonstrate comparably, it is important to identify these strengths as they can be harnessed to enhance the power force of your strategy, but more on that shortly.

One way of gaining assistance to identify your strengths or to validate your findings is to ask your customers what they think you excel at. You may be pleasantly surprised by their feedback. Another way of accessing insight into strengths is to identify what you are passionate about because passion is often linked to strengths.

Weaknesses are another area for review. Some weaknesses highlight areas that require focused strengthening due to the negative impact they will have on our strategic fulfillment. But other weaknesses highlight that which has little, if anything, to do with our ideal future state. These can often be fully discarded so that attention and resources are directed into our strengths. Many organizations lose their competitive advantage by focusing on too many areas. A lean operation demonstrates a direct focus toward strategic fulfillment.

Reflection Point

- In Table 2.3, list your organization's strengths and weaknesses.
- When you consider what you have written in the table, where should your attention and resources be directed?
- What operational areas would you consider weaknesses that possibly need to be let go of?

Table 2.3 Internal strengths and weaknesses

Our internal strengths are:	Our internal weaknesses are:

External Distinctions

Being distinctive is another driver of competitive advantage and while these distinctions may be small, they convey significant value to the end user.

From competitor analysis and the broader understanding of similar organizations we compete with, creating points of distinction is necessary to help our voice be heard in the crowded space we often find ourselves in. For example, those in the trade services space—whether they be electricians, plumbers, maintenance repairs, fire servicing—are generally known for being late to appointments without notification or not showing up at all. In creating an external distinction, a trade services company could offer a guarantee that if they do not advise the customer in advance they are running behind, the customer will receive the work done for free. Banks are known for not regularly communicating on the progress of loan applications to customers. If you were a mortgage broker, establishing a system to call your customers every three days to update them on progress would be a distinguishing factor. A builder I consulted with had as their distinguishing factor *luxury homes*. This immediately set them apart in a crowded marketplace where the majority were generic.

External distinctions can also be promoted from the identification of our strengths and weaknesses. A company in the technology engineering space capitalized on its major strength of reverse engineering. The owner mentioned most of his competitors would often start from the ground up to arrive at a solution whereas he would work backward from the problem, often correcting issues expeditiously. This strength was his external distinction. A construction company I was working with had design as their primary internal strength. The design team was exceptional at creating unique homes which then became their external distinguishing factor. In all their marketing material and sales conversations their design strength propelled prospective buyers to work with them. They stood out against their competitors simply from identifying this one distinction. From a strategic standpoint, this formed part of the top-down directive. Any decisions around the design of their homes had to fit within this framework. If, for example, they were contemplating building budget project homes, their previously formed strategy would have directed them otherwise, guarding them against becoming another builder in the same market as the majority of their competitors. This previously established competitive advantage continued to be the standard that all decisions were made against.

In all attempts to differentiate ourselves in the marketplace, the fundamental of it always comes back to what the customer perceives as high value. It is one thing to have a gimmicky distinction but if it is not seen as highly beneficial to the customer then a gimmick it remains without providing the traction that true value distinction offers.

Reflection Point

- What external distinctions could you create or capitalize on?

Pricing Advantage

Gaining a competitive advantage through pricing is foundational to gaining market share. A business may consider three main pricing strategies to optimize competitive advantage: under, premium, and comparative pricing. The success or otherwise of any individual pricing strategy is underpinned by lean business systems to ensure that the right strategy may be selected at the right time and adjusted according to the most salient and up-to-date information available, so that competitive advantage may not only be attained, but maintained.

1. Underpricing

Where this model is used, products are intentionally priced below that of the competition, providing the sales edge to price-sensitive consumers. This model is often adopted to gain significant market share to create high-revenue volumes. And while the products return a lower margin percentage to the organization, the financial return can be significant. This relies on an extremely accurate pricing model to ensure profitability and sustainability over the longer term. The other times this is used to advantage is when a company enters a competitive market with similar products and desires to gain early traction or in market downturns where a lower pricing model provides cash flow stability to ride out the short term. The essential component of underpricing is to ensure a thorough cost analysis has been completed to mitigate the chances of profit erosion and loss.

2. Premium Pricing

This is utilized when the products provided have clearly defined benefits that are perceived by customers to be worth the additional price. This model elevates a business above the common traffic where the majority of its competitors are fighting to gain customers through lower pricing. Staying clear of the dog fight on the ground, these organizations build their brand and repute through high-quality offerings and service. They charge more for their products and thus return a high profit percentage.

3. Comparative Pricing

This pricing model is designed to match the competition's pricing with one small twist. Pricing advantage is gained through *value differentiation*. The *above pricing* model mentioned prior charges additional for these differentiators; however, in comparative pricing when the benefits are clearly perceived by the customer, the decision is made easier. The price is the same, this product is more valuable, thus the choice is made.

While these different models can be adopted singularly, sometimes a mix of all three can be used to optimize competitive advantage. Butterfield Services (Aust) Pty Ltd are industry leaders in their development of lean systems, enabling enviable levels of business agility. Butterfield's pricing advantage lies primarily in the premium range, due to the transparency of data their customers can access via the user-friendly interfaces, dashboards, and reporting systems. This data transparency has created deep trust with their clients who, receiving greater value than from their competitors, are willing to pay a premium (specifically, for up-to-date information on their work orders and subsequent job's progress). However, when the need arises, their lean advantage enables Butterfield's to adapt and apply underpricing or comparative pricing models and they have the flexibility to do so. This is due to Shawn Butterfield and his team having taken a *systems-first approach* allowing them to operate with low overheads so that prices may be altered to win work, thus utilizing all three pricing models.

Reflection Point

- Of the three pricing advantage models, which one do you currently use?
- If you have never contemplated your pricing advantage, which one would be most applicable?

8. *Products, Revenue, and Demographics*

From everything we've reviewed on the strategic framework, it now comes to defining what products, markets, and revenue will form the future directive that will serve to guide us toward our ideal future.

A construction company, which I consulted, assessed their potential market and realized professionals and those who were wealthy empty-nesters made up the primary demographic of who their buyers were. They could then price accordingly and stay outside of the cut-throat pricing that many of their surrounding competitors were offering. Their profitability was significantly better than anything I had seen in construction and they did this simply by linking their products and revenues to an ideal demographic who were happy to pay extra for a wonderful home.

Recently I took my car to a mechanical services shop which is well known in our city. Their work and attention to detail were of a significantly higher standard along with the pricing. I was not price sensitive, but I was quality sensitive and for them, I represent one of their market demographics. In the highly competitive market of car servicing, this company has created a distinction in the market place by calling themselves a European car specialist. They have identified their product, core demographic, and charge accordingly.

The two examples I have provided here represent high-quality distinction to those customers who are willing to pay a premium price. Other business models will operate more on a high-volume low-margin model and again, this needs to be linked and marketed to the appropriate demographic. Project builders are one such business model that represents the high-volume, low-margin model. Their product, budget-priced homes, is focused on the demographic of lower income buyers and while each project returns a smaller profit, their high-volume model can create significant bottom-line results.

Some organizations have the potential of multiple revenue streams that can be considered throughout the strategic framework exercise. Industry associations, for example, while they are often focused on driving revenue resulting from membership, can also generate income from service providers, event attendance and sponsors, advertising space in their newsletters, and donations from those who believe in their cause. Short-sightedness can be avoided if we look broadly and creatively.

Reflection Point

- In Table 2.4, list three of your products with ideal revenue and target demographics. Revenue can be in terms of dollars or percentages.

Table 2.4 Products, ideal revenue, and demographics

Core products	Ideal revenue	Target demographic

9. Strategic Force

Part of the strategic clarification process is seeking to identify the enabler or power force within the strategy—that which leverages our strengths and insights, adding significant firepower to our efforts.

A story I heard as a young boy (when I grudgingly attended Sunday School with my family) was that of David and Goliath. Sometime in the 11th century BC, Goliath—a soldier who was over nine-foot-tall from the Philistine camp—challenged the opposing Israelite army. He wanted a man-on-man fight. The Israelite army was terrified, but this audacious shepherd boy David appeared out of nowhere and offered to kill Goliath. Once the King accepted, they dressed David in a coat of armor and bronze helmet for his head. He was handed a sword but had trouble moving. Removing the armor, helmet, and sword, and armed only with five smooth stones from the stream and his sling, he ran to Goliath, and using his slingshot, fired off one of the stones into the unprotected forehead of his opponent, killing him with just one shot.

David allowed a suit of armor to be placed on him but it took him out of his natural zone and slowed him down. He dared to revert to his natural *self.* He didn't use the weapon of another man but used the weapon he was familiar with—a slingshot and stone.

This story illustrates the power in simple things: The focus on opportunistic areas; the accuracy of aim; the use of a common commodity—a stone; not waging war by doing what everyone else does but by relying on personal strengths, skill sets, and courage. And it is important to note that without the slingshot, David would not have been able to defeat Goliath in the manner he accomplished it. The slingshot was the enabler, the force behind a common stone being fired.

When we find opportunity and aim accurately at those who represent our potential customers (even with common products), it is important to consider the strategic forces that can be harnessed—our slingshot. Strategic enablers are leverage points where more is done with less; where power is added to the common, much like the power of the wind behind the common canvas sail on a yacht. Here are some examples (some that I have also referred to in other contexts but are applicable here) to consider:

- A builder, known for higher priced homes, considers their *designs* as that strategic force.
- A construction-related company, also known for its higher pricing, says it is the way they build *relationships and care* for their customers that provides their power.
- A services company has invested heavily in *technology* allowing them to do significantly more with less.
- A *partnership* with a global company is the force for a manufacturer.
- An electrical company considers theirs to be offering *multiple solutions*, effectively a one-stop shop.
- When I was a mortgage broker, I was known as *the guy who could do loans that others couldn't. Creativity* was my power force. And when I first started consulting, many of my clients were connected to the gas mining boom. That was a powerful external force that propelled success.

Once these enablers are identified, they require focused attention and resourcing. Common items, such as a stone from the stream, the provision of a basic product, or the harnessing of an internal strength, can be transformed into powerful forces, driving us more efficiently toward our ideal future state.

Reflection Point

- What would you consider as your strategic force?

Uncongested Strategic Advantage

As mentioned previously, much of today's strategy work focuses on the gaining of strategic advantage over the competition. But sometimes, if we look beyond the competitive landscape there are wide open spaces in the marketplace, representing golden opportunities that few, if any, are pursuing. These are classed as noncompetitive advantage or which can be considered our uncongested strategic advantage.

Imagine with me for a moment: There is a centuries old, stone-walled city perched high on a hill in central Tuscany. The businesses there have for many years been servicing the needs of the residents within those walls with the cafes, restaurants, taxis, and others all having to compete against each other. They have promoted different points of distinction in the hope of attracting customers from the other businesses to themselves. On a warm spring morning, one of the business owners took a coffee break on the deck of a café that looked out over the city walls to the fields, small towns, and mountains beyond. Her mind started seeing new opportunities, silently mulling the question, "what if?" As she was day-dreaming she looked back at the hustle of the town, reflecting on the fact there was only limited supply and demand within the city walls. Grasping the power of this insight she determined that while she would maintain her current work in the city, she would begin researching opportunities outside of the city walls to create an uncongested strategic advantage.

While the story is apocryphal, it illustrates what many organizations are facing today: the same companies fighting for a piece of the pie from the same customers in the same region.

Uncongested advantage comes from thinking beyond the confines of the city walls. It means we think in terms of:

- Gaps in the current market not serviced by others or where there is a significant shortfall in providers (e.g., regional opportunities; those who provide financing arrangements for new customer purchases that are currently unavailable from traditional lenders).
- New business models that build on existing products and platforms (e.g., Uber, the iPhone, and the all-female gym, Curves).
- New products that have never been created before (e.g., the light bulb and telephones, the selfie stick, and Drones).

Uncongested strategic advantages become competitive over time as other organizations, observing the model and results from the forerunner, hop on the bandwagon with similar services. But in the case of Uber, while other ride-sharing platforms are now in direct competition, gaining the first position in the market creates a brand that gains first place in the mind and vocabulary of the consumer.

When we make the mistake of forecasting our future state on the products we have today and amplifying those with arbitrary growth goals, we miss the creative and innovative thinking that comes with thinking future first or, in strategic terms, our ideal future state. Looking to the uncongested spaces beyond is a powerful and sometimes growth-altering process that, if harnessed, can yield dramatic returns.

Reflection Point

- Where are the gaps and shortfalls in your current market that others have overlooked?
- Utilizing your strengths, what innovative products could you create that build upon current models but would be considered fresh and take you into uncongested territory?
- What have you observed in recent times where you thought "this product would really take off"?

Summary

The essence of this chapter has explained the necessity of creating a strategic framework that becomes the guiding directive against which all decisions are made, creating an efficient and fast movement toward our ideal future state. Strategy, as outlined in this chapter, contains:

- A compelling vision that is fashioned in a way that the *hearer* can see it.
- A purpose that engages the hearts and minds of our people and our customers.
- Values that represent the unwavering principles by which we will operate and be known for.
- Instead of arbitrary goals that reflect wishful thinking, our strategy contains critical and achievable objectives that propel us forward toward our ideal future state.

- Those critical issues that could present as obstacles in the achievement of our objectives.
- A method by which we will assess progress.
- The details of our competitive advantage that incorporate competitor analysis, our internal strengths and weakness, external distinctions, and our pricing advantage.
- An outline of the revenues that will be generated from our various products and the demographics they will appeal to.
- Uncongested or noncompetitive advantage highlighting those markets that are potentially wide open for us to gain an initial advantage within.
- Strategic force identification.

Endnotes

1. (Tregoe and Zimmerman 1980, p. 17).
2. (Rumelt 2017, p. 6).
3. (Hollo 2018, pp. 28–29).
4. (Weiss 1990, p. 6).
5. (For more about the confusion around Strategy and Planning see: Tregoe and Zimmerman. Top Management Strategy. What It Is And How To Make It Work. p. 23–27 Simon and Schuster New York 1980).
6. (Smithsonian National Air and Space Museum n.d.).
7. (Taylor 2020).

CHAPTER 3

Time Management

Just Where Did My Day Go?

Game Changer: *A primary root cause of inefficiency is the mismanagement of time. When we take control of our days through planning and methodical task execution; when we focus on outcomes rather than the hours worked, efficiency gains can be substantial.*

> It is wonderful how much work can be got through in a day, if we go by the rule—map out our time, divide it off, and take up one thing regularly after another. To drift through our work, or to rush through it in a helter-skelter fashion, ends in comparatively little being done. "One thing at a time" will always perform a better day's work than doing two or three things at a time. By following this rule, one person will do more in a day than another does in a week. (Mitchell 2014, p. 60)

Time is a finite resource with each having the same amount allocated to us. How is it that some achieve a whole lot more in their days and over their lifetimes than others? The management of time and tasks is foundational to this productivity.

My time management journey began some 35 years ago. I had taken on a new work role, entered a new relationship, and found I was being pulled from pillar to post, always feeling behind. An observant friend mentioned a foreign concept called time management. Due to my interest, he bought me a diary and over subsequent weeks taught me how to use it. I was hooked. My life changed dramatically, I was back in charge and from there I became a lifelong student of time management techniques. And while the time management thoughts and techniques that follow are essential for driving efficiency, I have learned that it is the outcomes achieved (at both a business and personal level), and not the length of time worked, that is the real game changer. And this all begins with understanding our daily energy.

Personal Rhythms

I think the age-old *do the hardest thing first* is a well-meaning but misdirected statement and should be rewritten to *do the hardest things when your energy is highest*. Each of us experiences peaks and troughs in our energy throughout our days and weeks. Some of us are early birds and some of us are night owls. Some do their best work in the mornings and some after midnight. Some are on fire first thing Monday morning while others feel like Tuesdays should be the start of the week. The key is understanding our energy flow and aligning our tasks accordingly.

A client I was working with mentioned several times that the office administrator came to work at 8 a.m. in a drowsy state and didn't really start working properly till late morning. I also came to understand they often hit their peak from mid- to late afternoon. I asked the business owner if there was any downside to the employee starting at 10 a.m. and finishing at 6 p.m. of which there wasn't. We talked to the administrator who loved the idea, made the change, and productivity automatically increased.

A common mistake in organizational life is placing the same start and finish times on all full-time employees with no regard to personal rhythms. If we want truly efficient, productive people, understanding and working with them to ensure they are operating within their peak hours makes sense. Daniel Pink in his book *When* explains:

> Human beings don't all experience a day in precisely the same way. Each of us has a "chronotype"—a personal pattern of circadian rhythms that influences our physiology and psychology. The Edisons among us are late chronotypes. They wake long after sunrise, detest mornings, and don't begin peaking until late afternoon or

early evening. Others of us are early chronotypes. They rise easily and feel energized during the day but wear out by evening. Some of us are owls others of us are larks. (Pink 2018, p. 27)

I learned to align my tasks to my energy several years ago when, after my divorce, and struggling through bouts of depression, I moved to a new city. It was just me, in a house, running my own business, and making the best of the situation. As a solo consultant, I always aim to spend about 50 percent of my time marketing, and at that time, I found it incredibly difficult to make phone calls to people I didn't know in order to set up sales appointments and then to show up to those meetings with full focus and energy. I learned to tune into the rise and fall of my energetic rhythms. As my self-awareness grew, I noticed that Mondays were lower energy days, and from late Tuesday morning through to Thursday night, my energy increased then started declining late Friday morning. I also noticed that between 11 a.m. and 2 p.m. and then from 3 p.m. to 7 p.m. were my daily peak energy times and then started rising again around 10 p.m. I learned to ride these energy waves, performing my most demanding work within the workday *highs*, and in the lower energy times, I would complete the more mundane or easier tasks. (Dancing was reserved for the evening peak.) If I had followed through on *do the hardest things first* it would have been ineffectual and disheartening.

Reflection Point

- What times during the day are you at your best?
- At what times does your energy drop off?

Once we gain insight into our daily peaks and troughs it is important to align our tasks accordingly. In Table 3.1, list your frequent tasks, the degree of concentration required, and the ideal time of day for completion, according to the rise and fall of your energy.

Once we have a greater self-awareness of our energy patterns, one way of ensuring we consistently operate within these rises and falls is to make a plan.

Table 3.1 Task, energy, and time-scheduling exercise

Primary tasks	Degree of concentration required	Ideal time for completion
e.g., Estimating	*High*	*9 a.m. to 1 p.m.*

Planning

Plan Tomorrow Today, Next Week This Week

Alec Mackenzie in his book *The Time Trap* writes: "*Planning* your day, rather than allowing it to unfold at the whim of others, is the single most important piece in the time management puzzle." He goes on to say,

> Nothing that you do in your attempts to better manage your time will be more valuable than this written plan. Without it, you are totally at the mercy of other people's demand on your time. With it, you always know where you are and where you should be, and equally important, you know what to do with new things that come along during the day—as they inevitably will. (Mackenzie 1990, p. 28)

While most would ascribe to the importance of planning, many show up for work, grab a coffee, possibly write a quick to-do list, and jump into their day. *Why would I take time out to plan when that time could be better spent knocking another thing off my list,* I hear people say. Although counterintuitive, planning time is not wasted time. As author and speaker Brian Tracy explains:

> The good news is that every minute spent in planning saves as many as ten minutes in execution. It takes only about 10 to 12 minutes for you to plan out your day, but this small investment of time will save you up to two hours (100 to 120 minutes) in wasted time and diffused effort through the day. (Tracy, Blog: Time Management n.d.)

When a disciplined planning approach is not a foundational habit and workloads increase, we tend to run faster, working longer hours just to keep up. Rather than sitting back, reviewing the work mountain in front of us, and planning ways to surmount it, in the running faster and working longer, waste occurs. We tire quicker, anxiety increases, task delegation effectiveness decreases, relationships suffer, and we are more prone to procrastination.

An important element of planning is to *plan tomorrow today* and *next week this week*. In this way, we are always working with a structured approach and can more clearly see and control the path ahead. The other aspect here is the importance of the *planning pause*. Regularly stopping to plan, even if for only two or three minutes to look at the next few hours, prioritize key tasks, and change our schedule as needed helps keep us focused and aligned on the outcomes we are seeking to achieve in the day. I have always found that the busier I get, the more often I stop for these planning pauses.

Those I have coached in shifting from a more spontaneous, unstructured approach to a well-thought through and planned methodology that aligns with the rises and falls of their daily energy have found significant gains in what they achieve. And one way to make the planning process easier and more efficient is to create a default diary.

The Default Diary

Routinizing our days and weeks, along with the mapping of tasks to our energy peaks and troughs is best accomplished through the creation of a default diary. Some tasks occur daily with others more infrequently.

The power of establishing the diary roadmap, and when followed, helps corral our focus and energies, saving us from thoughtlessly bouncing from task to task and the mismatch that comes from misaligned tasks to the rise and fall of concentration. Table 3.2 is an example of the default diary for an estimator over three days.

Table 3.2 The default diary

	MON 26	TUES 27	WED 28
6 AM	Exercise	Exercise	Exercise
7 AM			
8 AM	Travel	Travel	Travel
	Calls / Emails	Calls / Emails	Calls / Emails
9 AM			
10 AM	Management Meeting	Estimating	Estimating
11 AM			
	Estimating		
12 AM		Lunch	Lunch
1 PM	Lunch		Tender follow up calls
	Calls/Emails	Site visits / Client Meetings	
2 PM			
			Plan tomorrow
3 PM			
4 PM	Tender web review		Site visits / Client Meetings
	Plan tomorrow	Plan tomorrow	
5 PM	Travel home	Travel home	Travel home

In the default diary, we lay out the ideal working week and month. It contains our primary role responsibilities and provides a sense of focus, flow, and accomplishment. It forms the basis of a more disciplined and habitual process of working. In Table 3.2, we see the standard responsibilities along with preplanned white space. This provides flex to the day with the ability to schedule unexpected tasks or meetings as they arise. And while all of us have those days and weeks where the best-laid plans seem to disappear out of the windows of interruption and demand, being able to return to a default plan enables us to regain focus and control faster than if we don't have a roadmap, to begin with.

Once we have mapped our primary tasks with the rise and fall of our energies onto a default diary there are several factors to consider that increase focus and work outputs.

It's All about the Outcomes

Some years ago, a business colleague who was involved in real-estate sales contacted me and mentioned she had allocated three hours to call potential prospects with her goal of obtaining two new meetings to appraise the value of their homes. To her surprise, she achieved her goal within the first 30 minutes and then took herself for some pampering in the spare time she had created. While we may not all take ourselves for a manicure with the additional time we create, the power of this example was that my colleague was outcomes focused, and once she achieved her goal she moved on.

Time is the platform that outcomes and goal fulfillment are built on. When we consider the realm of sport, a team is allocated points for every goal they kick or shoot but, without these, they have merely used up their allocated time to go for a run. Not dissimilar to our days, without a focus on outcomes and kicking those completion goals, the hours become a run around the corporate field, busy but achieving little of worth. And to work efficiently, outcomes need to align with our strategic objectives, whether they be the broader organizational goals or departmental objectives, depending on the person's role.

In Table 3.3, I have demonstrated the difference between a generic labeled task and tasks that have specific outcomes.

Table 3.3 Tasks with outcomes listed

Generic task	Task with specific outcomes
Writing	Write 1,000 words
Bob's quote	Complete Bob Smith's quote and send
Call Sarah re. Social Media	*Finalize* Social Media work with Sarah
Follow up tenders	Call all outstanding tenders from last week
Write report	50 percent of ABC Ltd. report completed

Identifying task outcomes increases focus, resulting in higher outputs and speed of completion. Instead of feeling like we have had a day of just *doing stuff*, we start to see we are achieving tangible outcomes. This then assists in building momentum for the following day: one goal met is often the inspiration required to tackle the next one.

Using the default diary, we have already scheduled the best daily times for our tasks and have allocated approximate times to them. From here, we can then list the specific outcomes we want to achieve for those general tasks. Taking a day from the previous default diary for the estimator we can see how this can be integrated.

You will notice in the estimating section, as shown in Table 3.4, the person has listed the specific estimates they will work on. The flex time after lunch has been filled with completing a statistical report that was suddenly requested and they have also listed the names of those they are meeting onsite.

When we have a default diary as the baseline, we can then build on the platform, using it as our active diary, inserting primary tasks with their various outcomes alongside the time allocated for the task. It also provides the ability to batch similar tasks into preestablished blocks of time.

Batching and Blocking

A client said it this way: "I was working on a quotation and when the mail arrived I opened it. I noticed an error on the phone bill, called the company which took almost an hour, and am now well behind on my quote submission." This was a case of spontaneous and unplanned task management.

Table 3.4 *Default diary with outcomes*

	TUES 27
9 a.m.	
10 a.m.	Estimating: *complete Acme, Smith & Co; review request from Jones and Sons*
11 a.m.	
12 p.m.	Lunch
	Finish Stats report
1 p.m.	
2 p.m.	Site visits/client meetings: meet with Bob and Tim at Janarh Construction site
3 p.m.	
4 p.m.	
	Plan tomorrow
5 p.m.	Travel home

Batching and blocking are the batching or grouping of similar tasks into blocks of times and it is within these allocated periods that all related tasks are completed. The story above illustrates that if this manager had been working to a plan that allocated a specific block of time for quotation-related matters and another block of time where all administrative tasks were completed, it would have kept them singularly focused. They would have been more likely to get the quote submitted on time and wouldn't have been an hour behind at day's end. Distractions such as phone bills are common and when our days are unplanned and our work undisciplined, inefficiency is the result.

Task Identification for Batching—The Easy Way

Over the coming week, write down every unique task you do. At the end of the week, allocate these to their relevant categories. So if, for example, you have completed numerous marketing tasks, these would all be batched into one or more blocks of *Marketing* time in your diary. Once you have documented this you can create your default diary based on these categories while being mindful of the rise and fall of your energy— where you ensure you are doing the most challenging of these tasks in your peak times. You want to ensure you are completing similar tasks within the relevant category at the same time. This provides clarity of focus, greater levels of output, while minimizing distractions.

Task Identification for Batching—The Detailed Way

Joseph, a project manager, was struggling with always feeling behind. His days were a blur of tasks, calls, and meetings that left his mind spinning and weary at day's end.

For two weeks I had him keep a record of everything he did in 15-minute increments which included every incoming and outgoing phone call. At day's end, he would then color-code every individual task that related to specific categories: quotations, ordering, client liaison, supervisor calls, project planning, and so forth. Over a two-week period, the data he collated highlighted, among other things, that his quotation work was happening at random times, wherever he could fit it in. When preparing quotations, interruptions heighten the probability of errors. Get one part of the pricing wrong and you can lose your shirt on one job. It was critical in his case to batch all of these quotation times into focused blocks of time. We reviewed how much time he had spent on quotations along with how many were still outstanding. This gave us a clearer indication as to how much time should be allocated every week. We then blocked these times out on his diary and to increase his focus at these appointed times, I had him hand his mobile phone to the receptionist (much to his discomfort). Just this one change in his schedule significantly increased his quotation outputs along with his accuracy.

If you perform this 15-minute incremental time analysis for yourself, I recommend the following:

- Document your tasks at the time and be as precise as you can. Don't leave it till day's end.
- Ensure each task is assigned its relevant category.

- Document every interruption.
- Make notes as to where you could have done better or things that require changing moving forward.

At the end of two weeks, do the following:

- List the categories you have defined.
- Add up the time taken over the two weeks for each category. This will provide an estimate as to how much time should be allowed for each.
- Look for task patterns. An example would be when you receive the most number of incoming calls. Understanding patterns will assist you when planning the flow of your day.
- Reflect on the data in front of you. What is it telling you? How can you take this information and transform it into a more routined methodical process?
- Create a default diary with the information you have and begin the process of working to it, adjusting as you go.

Scheduling Interruptions

Batching and blocking also relate to interruptions. Leaders often comment on how much of their day is interrupted by unexpected incoming requests in the form of calls, e-mails, staff, and client requests. Most requests are not urgent and can generally be responded to within a few hours if not the following day. But we tend to immediately respond to everything that comes our way. Busy and reactive somehow make us *feel* like we are productive, but the truth is these interruptions reduce our efficiency, flow and resulting productivity.

A general manager I worked with spent most of his days responding to incoming calls and was unable to focus on any one task for any length of time. I had him analyze his daily phone calls over a one-week period and the data showed he was receiving, on average, 80 calls per day. We grouped these calls into categories of callers and then we started a re-route process. He set up a structure where most of his staff were given a *point person* to call: onsite workers were to call their supervisors; administration staff were to go direct to the office manager; and current customers were provided a new point of contact. Over the following weeks, his phone started to settle. He then started to get control of his day using the batching and blocking method and for the remaining incoming calls and requests that came his way, he scheduled the times he would check his messages and respond to them. He effectively scheduled what otherwise would have been interruptions and it changed his life and productivity dramatically. To limit interruptions consider the following:

- Give your mobile phone to someone else to answer or allow all calls to go through to voice mail.
- Set the landline to *do not disturb.*
- Turn e-mail alerts off and check them at allocated times every day.
- Close your door and communicate with others you are not available for the next period of time.
- When working on high-value tasks, remove yourself from the workplace traffic to complete these at home, in the boardroom, or in another location that promotes focus.

The To-Do List

While I am in favor of the default diary to provide (1) a visual map of the day and week, (2) an effective method for batching and blocking, and (3) the ability to align our tasks to rise and fall of our energy, it is important to address the to-do list as I know it is highly utilized by many.

The issue with the majority of lists I see on people's desks is they appear as a random collection of tasks rather than reflecting any prioritization or methodical order in which a person will complete them. Working on high-priority tasks in a focused manner is critical for high achievement. But when all tasks are treated as equal, we can find ourselves working on low-impact and easy tasks first and procrastinating on the harder higher priority tasks. The standard list, with no prioritization and no order, looks similar to this.

- Call James Gowrie.
- Write report for ACME.

- Arrange meeting with Sarah and Gary.
- Submit tender to Northern Star.
- Follow up CRM progress with Jane.
- Review last month's financials.

To more effectively utilize the to-do list is to ensure you are prioritizing the tasks and ordering them according to how you are going to move through them. A simple system is simply using an A, B, and C method: A, indicating highest priority; B, indicating secondary tasks; and C, only if you complete the A and B tasks. Once you have defined their priority, assigning a numbering system against the A, B, or C then provides you with an order from which to work from. Working in this way means you are always focusing on highest priority items while providing a sense of flow. If you don't get to the Cs that day, they can always be shifted to tomorrow and often they represent items that can be delegated or disregarded entirely. An ordered priority list is as follows.

- (C2) Call James Gowrie.
- (A2) Write report for ACME.
- (B1) Arrange meeting with Sarah and Gary.
- (A1) Complete and submit tender to Northern Star.
- (C1) Follow up CRM progress with Jane.
- (B2) Review last month's financials.

With the to-do list ordered as per above, it means that first thing you will work on (A1)—the highest priority task to be completed first. Once (A1) has been completed you would then move to (A2) and once all of the As have been completed you would then move on to the B tasks and similarly flow through them, being guided by the preset order. At day's end, it is then essential to transfer all uncompleted tasks to the following day's list or reassign to some future point. In this way, no uncompleted task gets neglected.

Prioritizing and ordering how we are going to move through our tasks increases our daily efficiencies enabling us to achieve more, with a higher degree of focused concentration and less time wasted.

Reflection Point

- What insights have you gained from this section on planning and what are the changes you will make from this point forward?

The Stop-Doing List and Delegation

Many of the leaders I have worked with have confided about their cynicism and fatigue in their roles. They feel overloaded from too much to do, too little time to do it in, are working longer, and for what? they say. One business owner mentioned he would drive to the office early, park around the corner and cry his eyes out before starting his day. It was all getting too much. Often in our work lives, tasks arrive onto our desks that we assume responsibility for. These can either be self- or other generated, but whatever their source, they easily mount up over time. It becomes essential then to frequently review the load we bear and the tasks we do, not only for our own well-being but also to ensure we are always working, whenever possible on high-value tasks.

In recent times I have been learning how to look after roses, ensuring that when they bloom, they do so at their full potential. One element hindering this potential is failure to manage their *water shoots*. These shoots grow at the base of the trunk and, if not regularly pruned, deplete the resources that would otherwise go into the main plant, thus retarding its growth. And water shoots are to a rose bush what secondary activities and tasks are to the organization and its leadership: they drain energy away from primary growth focus.

I mentioned the to-do list earlier but often overlooked is the stop-doing list (our very own water shoot list). This is a list that should be regularly completed to help identify that which is no longer relevant to our daily work and can be stopped entirely or delegated. It also relates more broadly to areas within our businesses that are not contributing directly to our ideal future state.

In completing the stop-doing list for our own tasks, some activities will be easy to identify but the more difficult ones are those driven by our internal needs and motivations. Some of the underlying reasons we find it hard to let certain things go are:

- Feeling guilty from saying no.
- A desire to please.
- Activity that makes us feel important.
- To be *seen* by others as busy and overloaded which fuels our self-worth.
- We enjoy certain tasks.

Part of the process of the stop-doing list is to identify those tasks that still require completion but can be delegated to others. The first area of effective delegation is related to those tasks you are currently doing that could *always* be completed by another person and can be part of a revised position description for them. These tasks can then become their ongoing responsibility, effectively removing it from your core role. The second area concerns those tasks we are still ultimately responsible for but can be completed by others. When a task lands on our desk the first question to ask is, "Who else can do this?" This is one of the most important questions we can be asking ourselves throughout our days. This starts the process of thinking beyond ourselves and is the basis of moving secondary tasks away from us, enabling continued focus on high-priority items. And don't overlook the junior people. Delegating both tasks and decisions to the most junior person in the organization, *along with the authority to carry them out*, allows everyone to use time more efficiently and effectively. This also benefits the junior person with the opportunity for faster progression into greater areas of responsibility.

There are four major reasons why delegation fails.

1. Failing to keep track of assigned tasks. Creating a system where we document what we have delegated, to whom, along with required completion dates keeps the assigned tasks from falling into the ether.
2. Delegation is confused with abdication. Effective delegation is supportive with accountability but abdication, on the other hand, is the assignment of tasks with no support or accountability.

Abdication effectively leaves the delegatee to their own devices and is often the reason why tasks go uncompleted and delegatory attempts fail.

3. Skill shortfalls. When tasks are delegated to those who do not possess the full skill set to execute the appropriate actions, delegation can fail at this point. When transferring tasks to others it is important to assess their capabilities ensuring where a skills gap does exist, there is a corresponding *upskilling* throughout the process.

4. Time. To delegate tasks to others means there is time involved in the transfer process. Sometimes, for the sake of speed, we opt to do the task ourselves. The ultimate goal of effective delegation, however, is the full reassignment of secondary tasks—where those tasks bypass us in the future—and taking the time now, to delegate to others while upskilling them in the process yields significant future returns.

Reflection Point

- What tasks are you currently doing that, if you stopped them completely, would have no negative consequences whatsoever?
- What tasks can you completely transfer to others?
- What activities do you need to incorporate into your schedule that will assist in faster progression toward your strategic objectives?

Write It All Down

Many attempt to keep lists and schedules in their heads but the trouble is, when the mind fills, things get forgotten. Given the pace of business and the changing nature of our days, not writing notes can amount to negligence.

On a consulting assignment, I met with the managing director who told me his priority for my work in the coming weeks was to focus specifically on one of the divisions within the company. After he gave me that directive, I went straight into interviewing 30 of his employees over the following three days. The information I received from these interviews in such a short space of time overloaded my brain and, because I hadn't written the prior directive down, it disappeared from my memory. He graciously pulled me up on my oversight to which I quickly made a course correction but it was the failure to write it down that was the cause of my mistake.

The business owner of a mining company called his project supervisor, directing him to check the dimensions of a certain product they were installing in the next few days. The supervisor failed to write it down and then failed to remember. The product was wrong, the job was delayed for five hours, and the onsite workers, having no further work to do, were sent home. The costs associated with this error were significant and it all came from not writing the directive down.

While writing everything down is important, it is the system we use with the daily planning and review time that brings it all together. A person I was coaching on time management told me that he was using six methods to keep track of his tasks which consisted of two notebooks, a diary, a tub in the back of his car for paperwork, and writing on his hand and leg. (I loved his honesty.) While he was writing most things down, the system he was using meant there were gaps everywhere. Combined with no disciplined planning time, he was, in his words, *all over the place.*

Writing everything into one system that is easy to use and accessible wherever we are, combined with daily review and planning, means the chances of forgetting are negligible.

Summary

The management of our time and related tasks is at the heart of personal efficiency. Time management is about:

- Working from increased self-awareness as to the rises and falls of our energy.

- Incorporating a disciplined planning approach where we constantly plan tomorrow today and next week this week.
- Focusing on the outcomes we need to accomplish.
- Batching similar tasks into blocks of time and working with a singularity of focus.
- Scheduling our interruptions.
- Re-routing tasks away from us through effective delegation.
- Seeking to always be working on high-value tasks.
- Pausing at times to reflect on what we should no longer be doing and create the stop-doing list.
- Ensuring we write everything down and have one system where no important task goes missing.

Time and task management, as I have found, is a lifelong subject to study and experiment with. There is not necessarily a right or wrong way but it is important to trial various techniques and methods until you find a way that is your way (what works best for you). When we manage our days and tasks stringently, we achieve more in less time resulting in a less-stressed existence. We will be nicer to be around, being more fully present with those we connect with and live with. Effective time management combined with working on high-value tasks that are aligned to our strategic objectives not only increases our own efficiencies but impacts the broader organizational efficiencies.

CHAPTER 4

People

People Who Feel the Love, Show the Love

Game Changer: *We often overlook our people as a major factor to our success and the more we invest in them, the more they feel valued, the more they will shine and perform efficiently.*

People are complex beings. If we think of what makes up the person we could look at areas such as physical, emotional, intellectual, spiritual, ego, their history—the good and the painful, dreams and ambitions, values, beliefs, behaviors, purpose, interests, talents and innate gifts, self-image, personality, obsessions, addictions, standards and principles, internal drivers and motivators. With that list, no wonder people issues for management are cited as one of their highest challenges. And just as each snowflake is different from the next, so too is each person to their neighbor.

Valuing the People We Lead

I was in the process of creating a proposal for managing director, David O'Brien, of Doboy Cold Stores when I asked him what our work together would likely contribute to the bottom line. I will never forget his passionate response: "I am not interested in a financial return. My team means everything to me and if they will be better off from your work then that is all I want." I did not have to ask for further clarity. In an introductory e-mail that David sent to his team on April 6, 2016, he said,

> Dear all … Doboy's greatest assets are the truly wonderful people, who make up the Doboy Team. I genuinely regret that the complexity of my role has prevented me from engaging with

my co-workers to the level that I would have preferred. I am keen to understand what makes you feel great about your job, what motivates you, and, of course, what frustrates you. To help me to begin to redress this situation, I have taken the decision to invite Ray Hodge, an expert in this field, to visit Doboy over the weeks ahead ... I have asked him to establish what we are doing right and to identify areas where we could do better ... Please consider this as a great opportunity to make Doboy an even better place to work!

Our greatest assets are the truly wonderful people ... This was not a glib statement parroted off by a well-meaning business owner. He lived and breathed having individuals working for him who were happy and productive in their work. He wanted to see them develop as individuals and in their respective work roles. And as I subsequently met with all of the people throughout his organization, the respect each had for him was significant and interestingly, one of the suggestions for improvement (from his people) was they wanted to see more of him. You do not get much better than that from employees.

One business owner told me he wanted his employees to leave their personal baggage at the front door before they entered the office. In all my time consulting I have never seen any bags in the conceptual front office baggage area. The reality is that people do bring their personal life into the workplace to varying degrees, as James, a human resources manager, discovered.

When I first met James, he was working at a commercial joinery company in his HR role. Fast paced, forceful, results oriented, he was singularly focused on productivity. His assistant on the other hand was a fun and bubbly person who would happily breeze into the office after the weekend and with a big smile ask him how his weekend was. He frustratingly said one day, "I don't give a f**k about what she did on the weekends nor do I have the time for her to ask me what I did for the weekend. When she gets to work I expect her to go straight to her desk." Leading people different from him and acknowledging the personal aspects of the people he was responsible for was a challenge.

Six years later, I received a call from James to do another project for a company where he was now the operations manager. Interviewing each of his direct reports, I was amazed by the terrific things they were saying about his leadership. "Was this the same man I knew six years ago?" I thought to myself. I was intrigued. Subsequently, we met and I reminded him of what he had demanded of his previous assistant many years ago and asked what had transpired since, to create such positive feedback from his people. He mentioned that sometime after I had worked with him, he started a new role on a mine site in Western Australia. From the initial conversation with me (about his assistant) and the coaching work we had done together, he had spent a lot of time working hard to adjust his approach with people. The tipping point came when he casually asked one of the employees how their day had been and the man, opening up, explained that on the previous night he had considered over-dosing. Life was too painful, too dark. Taking James by surprise, this wasn't a conversation he had expected. The man had placed a lot of faith in him by sharing this and James knew his response at that time was crucial. He asked the man why he was feeling that way, what had brought him to that point, how he could support him best. James subsequently went to several counseling sessions with the man and the counselor, pulling him aside at the end of one of these, told him that had he not asked the man that simple question about how his day was going, the counseling sessions would never have happened. It had been that dire.

James became more effective in his management of others from the realization that people matter; that valuing, caring, and loving them for *who they are* provided the foundations for bringing the best out of them. While the rest of this chapter is largely devoted to how to better understand and work with our team members, providing various frameworks and performance improvement techniques, the demonstration of valuing others through genuine interest cannot be underestimated.

A Framework for Understanding People

Social Styles

Most leaders are not trained in psychology and a basic framework for understanding people, for the non-psychologist, can be extremely helpful.

One such framework I have found to be incredibly useful and easy to use is the social style model as published by Robert H. Bolton and Dorothy Grover Bolton in their book *Social Style/Management Style*. Social styles are about *seen* behaviors, rather than *unseen* personality. As the authors' state: "Behavior refers to everything a person does that is directly observable. It includes the whole gamut of verbal and nonverbal actions."[1] They also say that "Social style is about the consistent patterns of actions that a person uses when in the presence of other people."[2]

If you reflect on those you have interacted with this past week, some might have exhibited quite expressive behaviors; some would have seemed to be a *closed book* and difficult to converse with; others more direct and outspoken while some were more detailed and analytical. While each of us tends to have a default style—a general *way* we present and operate—different environments also evoke different behaviors. A person might be more directive at work but at home, their assertiveness lowers. Some are more emotionally controlled in the work environment but may exhibit more expressive communication when they go out with friends (especially after six beers). All of us express different styles at different times and therefore it can be extremely limiting to categorize people as a *high D*, a *peacock,* or any other form of a label. Labeling ourselves and others create artificial barriers along with excuses for nonchange or performance. But when we view these models as tools for understanding the *behaviors* we exhibit in different environments, along with using them to appreciate and work with others, they can be extremely useful.

The Two Elements of Social Styles

At its most fundamental level, the social style model presents two primary dimensions that help us understand a person's behavioral style.

1. The degree to which someone is or is not demonstrating *assertive* behavior.
2. The degree to which someone is or is not expressing a more *emotionally responsive* style.

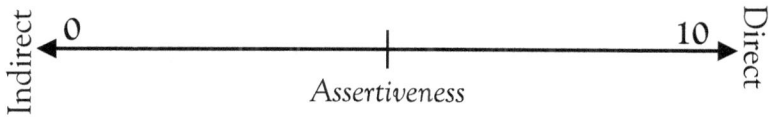

Figure 4.1 Social styles assertiveness axis

Figure 4.1 presents the degree to which someone is interacting with a more assertive, direct style. The lower the assertiveness factor the more likely the person exhibits a *sit-back*, less confrontational style who allows others to make decisions. The higher up the scale a person presents will be reflected in a more direct and confrontational behavior. They are more likely to take risks and control their environment and conversations.

Figure 4.2 represents the degree of emotional responsiveness.

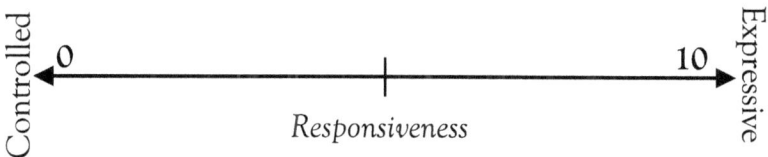

Figure 4.2 Social styles responsiveness axis

When someone is less responsive they exhibit behaviors that tend to be more reserved, demonstrate emotional control, are more process oriented and factual, whereas further along the scale, the person tends to be more outgoing, socially engaging, and feelings oriented.

Reflection Point

- In the workplace, what level of assertiveness, out of 10, do you exhibit most of the time? ____/10
- In the workplace, what level of responsiveness, out of 10, do you exhibit most of the time? ____/10

The Social Styles Quadrant

The two axes when combined create a quadrant model that assists in further understanding the typical behaviors a person exhibits. Having completed the reflection point above for ourselves we can then translate this onto the relevant axes as demonstrated in Figure 4.3.

The example below reflects someone who rated themselves 8 out of 10 on both the responsive and assertiveness scales. This then places them in the lower right-hand quadrant. Each of the quadrants is designated an identity that helps us further understand the social style someone operates in as Figure 4.4 illustrates.

Each of the social styles listed in Figure 4.4 has associated behaviors, goals, dislikes, orientation—whether people or task focus—and the speed at which they are more likely to operate. Understanding these provides greater insight into those we connect with enabling us to focus on what is important to them as shown in Table 4.1.

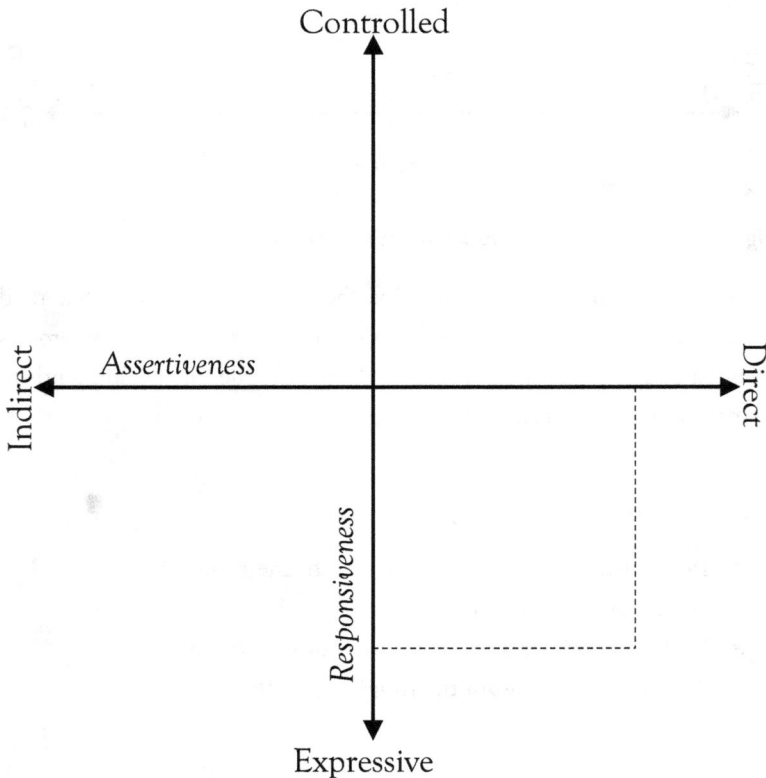

Figure 4.3 Style identification

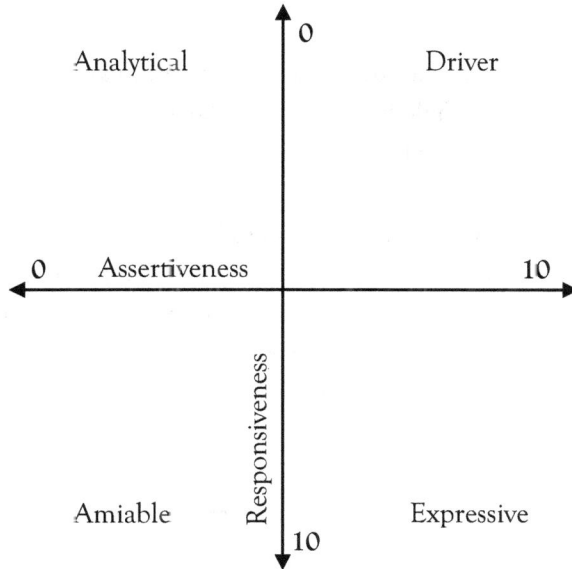

Figure 4.4 Quadrant names

Table 4.1 Social styles summary

Style	Typical behaviors	Major goals	Dislikes	Orientation	Speed
Analyt-ical	Methodical Reserved Logical	Accuracy and order	Lack of factual detail	Task	Moderate
Driver	Direct Decisive Independent	Results Control	Indecision Tardiness	Task	Fast
Expres-sive	Extroverted Spontaneous Vivacious	Recognition and fun	Detail Routine	People	Fast
Amiable	Accommo-dating Supportive Calm	Personal connection Stability	Constant change	People	Moderate

Style Flex

To effectively connect with others, it is important to start with *who they are,* adapting our default behaviors accordingly to their style. This is known as *style flex.* Again from *Social Style/Management Style*:

> Style flex is a way of taking responsibility for the results you achieve through your behavior. It is communicating in a way more readily understood by and more agreeable to persons of another social style. It involves using some body language and wording that match the preference of the person whose style you are flexing to. (Bolton 1984, p. 55)

To help understand this further here are some scenarios that often occur in the workplace.

1. Relating to the Analytical
   - Situation: The boss is an analytical type who values facts and details; however, she gets frustrated when her sales manager, an expressive type, comes with flowery optimistic stories of how their week was. Her manager takes twice the amount of time that is needed and comes unprepared with no data to support their activity.
   - Effective connection: The sales manager would improve their communication effectiveness by taking time to prepare, cut out the small talk, and attend the meeting armed with a detailed report. All conversation needs to be factual and based on the sales data.
2. Relating to the Driver
   - Situation: A customer walks in and quickly states a problem he has with the machine he purchased recently, looking at his watch in the process. The customer service representative is more the Amiable type. They seek to gain a personal connection with the customer, asking him what he was planning to do on the upcoming weekend.

This frustrates the customer and says he doesn't have all
day to get a resolution.

- Effective connection: Upon detecting the speed and
directness of the customer's speech and the fact he
looked at his watch is enough to understand this person
is probably a driver and the need to get straight to
the point.

3. Relating to the Expressive

- Situation: The receptionist is an Expressive girl, who loves
to laugh and engage with customers over the phone and
in her interactions with colleagues. Her manager, however,
is more the Analytical, who dislikes the amount of time
she takes *fluffing* about and the constant laughter he hears
coming from that department.

- Effective connection (or in this case, Effective Leadership):
As difficult as this is for the Analytical manager, to bring
the best out of her means adapting to her style to connect
with her. And it does mean smiling, talking about their
weekends and fun things, not just work-related activity. If
her work outputs are suffering due to her style then a focus
on reorientating her to the related performance metrics
for her role would be important. However, in many of the
Expressive people I have observed, the happiness factor
is *part* of their productivity, and being able to appreciate
their way is important. Moreover, they are a delight to be
around and customers appreciate a phone being answered
with a happy voice.

4. Relating to the Amiable

- Situation: The general manager is a softly spoken,
moderately paced Amiable type who values her people
and takes time to connect with them. She is strategic in
her thinking and tends to make decisions slowly rather
than the business owner who, as the Driver type, wants
fast instinctive action with less time taken for personal
conversations.

- Effective connection: If the business owner took a step back and reflected on the fact that the general manager is getting the required results even though she is going about it in a different way to what they would, this would help alleviate their frustration. Along with this, it would be important that when meetings are scheduled with the general manager, the business owner schedules more time to converse personally while reducing the speed at which they think and speak.

A manager I was coaching started experimenting with style flex. He was more the Analytical type who naturally got straight to the detail. In a meeting with a client who was his direct style opposite, the Expressive, he let go of his task and detail orientation and, as much as he felt he was wasting time, took the detours of personal engagement—talking about the man's family, hobbies, and weekend pursuits (which the client was initiating), while ensuring he covered only the main points about the work the client required. He reported back that the personal connection gained with the client significantly enhanced the potential of future work they would do together as referenced by the client themselves.

Whatever our sphere of connection—whether they be in a work-related area or the personal arena—when we appreciate that each is different and when we honor those differences by flexing our behaviors accordingly, the benefits can be significant.

Reflection Point

In Table 4.2, list the social style of three people that are different to you along with the style flex required by yourself to more adequately connect with them.

Table 4.2 Style flex requirements

Person's name	Their likely style	Style flex required

Working with Values

Another factor in helping us understand and to work effectively with others is the understanding of people's values. Values reflect the priority of our preferences to which we allocate time, resources, and energy, in direct relationship to their preference ranking. There are many areas we as humans value and, for the sake of brevity, I have listed in Figure 4.5 eight life areas to demonstrate how for one person they could be prioritized on the value ladder.

For this person, whose top three values are career, family, and health, they will spend much of their time, energy, and money toward these values. As the value prioritization drops so too will the drive to fully invest in and improve these areas of their life. Where this is important in bringing the best out of others is that when we as leaders understand a person's highest values we can often move them in extraordinary ways.

As part of a consulting project, I was requested to work with an account manager to improve his sales performance. As I met with him over

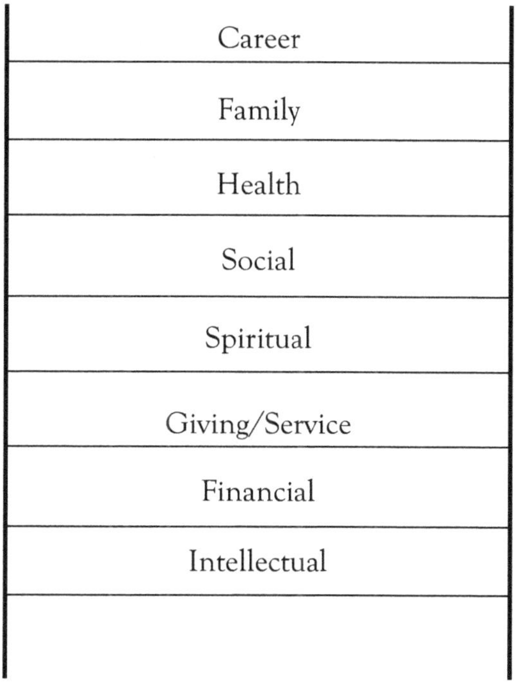

| Career |
| Family |
| Health |
| Social |
| Spiritual |
| Giving/Service |
| Financial |
| Intellectual |
| |

Figure 4.5 The values ladder

subsequent weeks, I came to understand that family was his highest value. It was relatively easy to gain access to this insight as in every conversation there was always some communication about his wife and two children of which he spoke passionately. When it came to his sales career, this was not a priority. He was simply at work to make a living so he could support and be with his family. Instead of first heading down the standard track of helping him organize himself, categorize his prospects, and learn sales techniques, I went another route. I asked him what he would like to do with his family in the coming year. He immediately responded that he would like to take them to Disneyland and also mentioned if he had the money, he would send his children to a private school. At this point, I opened up his sales budget and at the top, plugged in the Disneyland costs along with the annual school fees. I then demonstrated the relevant commission levels that were aligned to the sales targets he had to meet so he could make his family goals achievable. I remember vividly when the *lights came on* within him. In a moment, he saw that his work, instead of being a daily sales trudge that took him away from his family, was now the means of achieving his family's goals. Once the connection was made—linking one of his lowest values (his career), to his high value of family—he became motivated and the sales training I subsequently completed with him was incredibly easy. He was hungry to learn. And for his employer, he met the required sales budget.

The above story illustrates that when we understand our people and what their internal drivers are—the values and goals they are driven toward—we can often link their daily work to these highest values. And to ascertain people's highest values, we first have to be interested in the person and second, it is often through conversations we learn what is important to them. Some leaders are extremely uncomfortable with this; however, the more we get to know the *whole person*, as opposed to just the *work person*, the greater the potential for performance increases.

Reflection Point

- What are your top three values?
- Thinking of a person you work closely with, what would you perceive their top three values to be?
- How could you more effectively link their work to their highest values?

Different Equals Different

"Why can't she just get out of her analytical head every now and again …?"

"I dislike that he always leaves on time because of…"

"He always ensures he takes a lunch break but I'm so busy I can't afford to. That really annoys me about him."

I have heard these and a thousand variances from leaders about their people. While high expectations and standards for employees are essential, the expressed grievances from leaders about their people are often a reflection of themselves. This is a case of paradigm projection where we project onto others who we think they should be, based on who we are, forgetting they are unique individuals. A case in point was a supervisor who frustratingly mentioned that one of his team showed high potential, but as much as he tried to push him forward to take on further responsibilities, the employee dug in. He did not want to progress further because he simply wanted to come to work, make his money, and go home to pursue his passion for music. His music passion was a high value which wasn't valued by his supervisor. This created a major difference between them and while the supervisor had a goal for his team member, it wasn't a shared goal. They were simply different.

Often, and even though we wouldn't say it out loud, we perceive *different equates to wrong*. If they think and work differently to me then surely they have to lift their game, but I've come to see that different doesn't necessarily equal wrong, it can simply mean that *different equals different*. When we grasp this understanding, it causes us to shift from more autocratic leadership styles to a more adaptive style, working with people according to *who they are* rather than *what we think they should be*. In Table 4.3, I have outlined just how different two people can be who work side by side.

You can see that for both Raquel and Peter, if they do not have a deep appreciation for each other's differences and work in a way that honors those differences, their time at the office will be quite the challenge. Here is an example of how they might adapt their approaches to enhance working together.

- For Raquel, if she understood that family is Peter's highest value and created a results-based work life for him (as opposed

Table 4.3 Different equals different

Life areas	Raquel—vice president	Peter—general manager
Values	Career and money	Family
Skills	Organization and strategy	Finance and organization
History	No loss in her life	Loss of a previous wife to cancer and a child to suicide
Social styles	Dominant and direct	Amiable and easy going
Personality	Extroverted	More introverted
Self-image	High	Low
Beliefs	Long hours are a sign of commitment	Results, not time is what counts
Corporate goals	20% annual growth	Lowering employee attrition
Personal goals	Get to the top no matter how	Being a loving provider for his family
Motivations	Expansive public perception	The personal well-being and engagement of his team
Interests	Work and more work	Baking bread and pizza

to time based) while nongrudgingly accepting he is going to be leaving on time every day, she is more likely to get outstanding results.

- If Peter helps Raquel to get into the public square more, approaches her in a direct manner while ensuring he focuses on sales growth with regular updates to Raquel, he will raise the value of his contribution (in her eyes) significantly.

In both these examples, Raquel and Peter have managed to gain insight into their counterpart, performing in a way that serves the other while working toward the corporate goals. Understanding, appreciating, and working with others according to who they are is a powerful force for growth, harmonious relationships, and workplace satisfaction.

They're Doing the Best They Can

I am often surprised how a few words at the right moment in time can have a life-changing effect. Reading Brené Brown's book *Rising Strong*, I came across the following words: "We're all doing the best we can."[3]

These words reverberated deeply within me and began a dismantling process. They shifted me from a more controlling and demanding person to one who saw that people were a product of their histories and nature's wiring, rather than being wrong, resistant, or hopeless. Sure, there were some great people I had worked with and had as friends but upon reflection, I liked them because we shared commonalities. But God help those who were different to me. They were straight out *wrong*. This concept dramatically shifted my executive coaching work, helping me see in particular that underperforming people needed to be *worked with* rather than *yelled at*. It caused me to start with *where they were*, doing the journey with them to *who and where they could be*, and surprisingly, the results have been startling. When we treat our team members as multifaceted human beings who generally are doing the best they can, and when we choose to lead from beside rather than barking from afar, we stand a better chance of increasing our peoples' performance and efficiencies whilst decreasing our own anxiety and frustration in the process.

From Low Performance to High Performance

If we begin with the assumption that our people are generally doing the best they can then it makes sense to start the improvement process from where they are, working *with them* to help develop them to where they need to be. While group training has some use and is often general in nature, tailor made, individual development with accountabilities that relates specifically to the performance shortfalls for the employee is more effective. One such tool I developed that has proven to be an efficient means of moving people along the performance development pathway is shown in Table 4.4.

In the example shown in Table 4.4, the required improvements relate to an employee who never achieves advanced scheduling and is regularly two days behind.

1. Improvement Objective. In the first column, this objective is very specific in what outcome is expected—*jobs booked three days in advance*. You will also notice the completion goal of 90 days.

   I have used this here as an arbitrary figure and it can be any time frame the manager sees as reasonable. The purpose of the time frame is to provide focus and intention to drive faster progress.

Table 4.4 Improvement matrix example

Improvement objective	Improvement steps	Progress evaluation *Manager's* score	Progress evaluation *Employee* score
Increase scheduling efficiency with jobs booked 3 days in advance	• Noninterrupted scheduling time is to happen between 7 a.m. and 10 a.m.; 2 p.m. and 4 p.m.	60%	80%
Completion goal: 90 days	• Daily review of all uncompleted jobs and schedule their completion	30%	10%

2. Improvement Steps. These demonstrate the specific actions the employee is required to implement throughout the process. Rather than just *telling* the employee where they need to arrive at, the specific actions provide tangible and incremental steps they can follow and are best worked through with the employee to gain their ownership of the process.

3. Progress Evaluation. This section is completed by both employee and manager at regular intervals to assess progress. You will notice in Table 4.4 that both of them have scored differently according to their perspective, which often happens. When these discrepancies appear, it allows both parties to share their opinions as to progress and the accompanying challenges, helping them both arrive at a game plan for the coming period of time.

The critical component of this improvement process is ensuring the manager is supporting the employee in the changes. It's easy to request from the employee to have uninterrupted time for scheduling (as in Table 4.4) but if the employee has spent the last 20 years working with their door open and responding to every interruption that comes their way, the manager then needs to address the time management issue in the process of driving the improvement.

This incremental, staged process is one of the most simple, yet powerful methods of improvement I have created. For an employee to understand the specific outcomes required of the improvement process with ongoing support and accountability dramatically enhances the results. Our people first need to understand *what* they need to be doing and second the outcomes or metrics that will define if they are fulfilling those responsibilities.

Position Descriptions and Performance Measures

I started an improvement project for a company and asked one of the employees for their position description. They said they didn't have one and that when they had initially asked the executive for one, they were told the *title* of their role was their position description. I laughed and asked, "so how do you know what to do?" to which they responded, "Oh, I've been making it up as I go." The number of companies that have not clarified the responsibilities of individual roles is numerous. If you do not have position descriptions, get on to it immediately. It will be a big difference to people working efficiently.

If there are position descriptions, while most have a list of responsibilities, the noticeable missing component is performance metrics that relate to the specific responsibilities. As an example, two of the responsibilities of a service manager might include:

1. Quoting as required.
2. Scheduling of the service team.

These are general and in their current form are immeasurable. My question to leaders is "how do you know the person is performing these responsibilities and how do they know they are performing?" What's missing is performance measures as shown in Table 4.5.

You can see from the following example that both the manager and the employee know exactly how to measure performance. When these are absent, role efficiency is often decreased. A person I was coaching within an administration team had as their primary task the responsibility of invoicing and through the process, I discovered they were three months behind. While the employee was fulfilling their fundamental responsibility of invoicing daily, with no performance metric, they meandered their

Table 4.5 Performance measures

Responsibilities	Performance measure
Quoting as required	All quotes to be sent to the client within 3 days of initial inquiry with 24-hour follow-up
	A monthly minimum of $1.5 million in quotes to be generated
	25% conversion rate
Scheduling of the service team	Scheduling to be completed 3 days in advance
	Achieve a 90% productivity rate for the service team

way through their days, apparently busy but inefficient. Upon identifying this we established a performance measure of *invoices to be sent within five days of job completion.* Over the next few months, we then created daily invoicing goals to bring them back within the five days to which they achieved.

Performance measures can transform an organization in a very short space of time, providing clarity to individuals and teams while driving efficiencies from a more thorough understanding of the outputs required.

Right Person Right Role

Having the right people, operating in the right roles according to their social style and their corresponding skill sets, contributes significantly to the overall efficiency flow throughout the organization. But the wrong person in the wrong role has the reverse effect.

In one company, I was asked to *sort out* the receptionist/administration person. The information I was provided suggested they were great on the phone and customers loved them but their attention to detail in administrative tasks was severely lacking. I met with the person and quickly came to understand that at a social style level, they operated more in the expressive quadrant. If you review the social style quadrant back in Figure 4.4 you will notice the expressive behaviors are diametrically opposite to those with a more analytical behavior, which the role of administration requires. As the employee expressed what they enjoyed about their work and where the challenges were, anything to do with people they loved, but anything to do with the detail of administration they disliked. After speaking with the business owner, we created a new role for them that was primarily *people oriented* and then recruited someone else for administration. Both the employee and the administrative department increased their efficiencies as a result of the changes. I have seen expressive people in data entry roles; very shy, conservative, and introverted people in customer-facing roles; slower paced, routined, and inflexible individuals in roles where speed and adaptability are essential; fast-paced, direct, and results-oriented people in roles where they were required to do mundane routine work. While we can have the best systems and technology in the world, the wrong person in the wrong role or at a particular process point within a workflow impacts efficiencies.

One of my observations has been that leaders tend to home in on particular skills required for the role; forgetting this is just one of a number of suitability components. One other important attribute is teachability. The times I have come across stubborn, immovable employees is numerous and apart from driving leaders to despair they negatively impact organizations on multiple fronts. Teachable people are a gift and the more of them we have the easier it is to grow leadership from within and move people where we need them. I developed the expertise–teachability model (Figure 4.6) to portray the importance of this trait in relation to the level of *skills expertise* in the person.

Quadrant 1. The Poor Fit

The current lack of job expertise combined with little or no desire to learn makes forward progress challenging and time consuming for management. It does not mean there is anything wrong with the person; it's more likely to be explained by their place within the organization, or that the organization itself isn't a naturally good fit to inspire them to learn and grow. This type of person would probably be better placed elsewhere (perhaps in someone else's business). The arrows in this quadrant indicate training and coaching are required in both job-related expertise and personal teachability. The arrow pointing outwards suggests helping them depart could be the most mutually agreeable outcome.

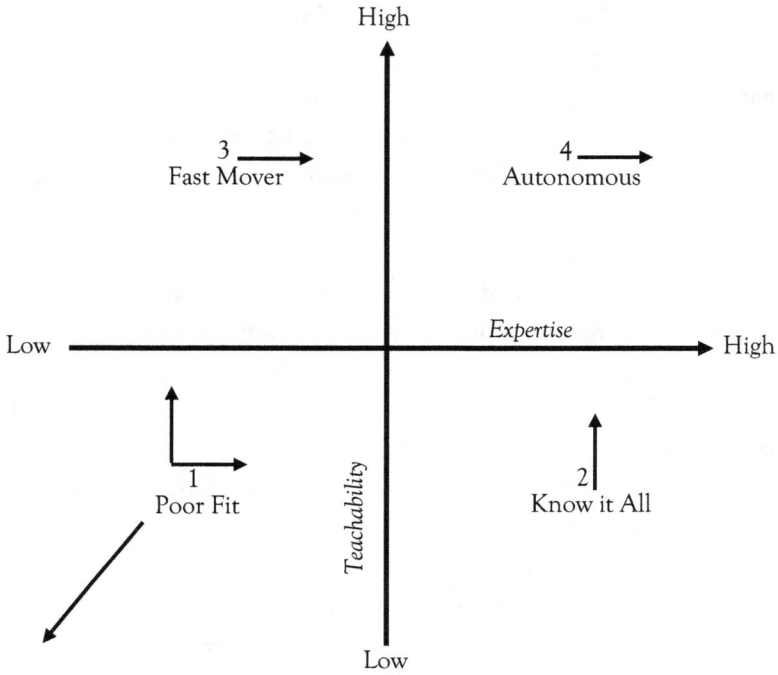

Figure 4.6 Expertise–teachability model

Quadrant 2. The Know-It-All

This team member (actually individual player) is highly competent in their work but their lack of teachability is reflected in resistance to change. They generally reject the notion that they could possibly improve; believing the organization revolves around them. The vertical arrow represents coaching is required in teachability.

Quadrant 3. The Fast Mover

This person may not have fully developed expertise in their role but because they are naturally higher on teachability they approach each day as an opportunity to develop new skills that will make them proficient in their job. This person is a "gift" within the organization and is the perfect recruit whether early or later in their career. Nurturing such an employee along the horizontal arrow via mentoring/training will foster even faster growth and promote loyalty.

Quadrant 4. The Autonomous

The combination of teachability and technical skill means this employee will meet and exceed the demands of their specific job requirements. People in this quadrant are likely to be innovators within the business, blessed with the insight and foresight needed to perceive and respond to change. This type of person can function autonomously and, to retain employees of this caliber, management needs to work with the person to identify meaningful ways to reward and sustain exceptional performance.[4]

The recruitment stage is critical to ascertain the right person for the appropriate role but often leadership shortcuts the process, especially when the labor market is tight. "Better we get anyone who can take the load now than waiting for the perfect person," I've heard it said, but frequently I have seen when companies shortcut the upfront process they pay for it (and often expensively) down the road. It is critical to have a highly streamlined recruitment process in place, and as part of it, ensuring you have a means of being able to understand the prospective employee's expertise, their teachability, along with the relevant social style.

Sometimes though, we have good people in existing roles where it becomes apparent over time they are not a perfect fit. When this is the case and for some reason you are unable to move them to a more suitable position, the improvement matrix in Table 4.4 mentioned previously in this chapter can be useful. While it is not a perfect solution it does help the manager and the employee identify areas of challenge and shortfalls with an incremental improvement pathway for them to work toward. Extra support and training are often required along with the redistribution of tasks to more suitable others wherever deemed appropriate.

Summary

People can be a very challenging aspect of leadership yet efficient people are a central part of the lean and competitive organization. To increase our effectiveness as leaders it is important to:

- Communicate that we value our people and that they are important, not only for the work they do but for who they are as a person.

- Ensure that the right people are in the right roles for them.
- Understand that everyone is different and the greater our ability to flex to their style the more effective we will be in our leadership of them.
- Bringing the best out of people starts with where the person is, taking them from where they are to where they could be, through supportive and incremental improvement.
- Document their roles, responsibilities with related performance measures, and hold them accountable for the achievement of such.

While people often represent some of the most challenging aspects of organizational life, they also can be one of the most rewarding.

Endnotes

1. (Bolton and Grover Bolton 1984, p. 4).
2. (Bolton and Grover Bolton 1984, p. 16).
3. (Brown 2015, p. 118).
4. This first appeared on www.rayhodge.com.au/blog and has been adapted for use here.

CHAPTER 5

Workflows

If It Ain't Flowin', It Ain't Efficient

Game Changer: *Efficient workflows are a critical component to the development and maintaining of internal lean operations which, in turn, like a river effortlessly flowing toward the sea, drives our competitive advantage out to the broader marketplace.*

"We don't need more profit, we just need order to our chaos," said one executive. "We have been on a plateau for eight years and need to get off it," said the partner of a professional services firm. "If we don't do something immediately the company is going to implode," said another owner from a manufacturing firm. These and many more statements like them have formed much of my efficiency work and processes, which this chapter is built on. While there are many in-depth and analysis-driven books on this topic, this chapter provides practical applications which can be applied immediately. I will be sharing the fundamental processes I use for organizations that struggle with efficiency in their workflows to release greater amounts of productivity, order, and profits.

When flow is hampered, the effects can be significant. The five major ones I most often encounter are:

- Dissatisfied customers.
- Unhappy staff with high attrition rates.
- Too many staff.
- Low revenues, high expenses, with low profitability.
- Cash flow issues.

These are simply external outcomes from internal issues, with work-flow efficiencies often being a major contributor. The one underlying principle is: clear the blockage to allow for increased flow through the pipeline.

Don't Forget the Customer

One of the factors most often missed in creating a lean operation is what our customers desire. Given our companies exist for the customer, consideration of what is most important *to them* is central to the process. Workflow efficiencies completed in the absence of *what does the customer want?* can result in wonderful internal efficiencies with external customer frustration. A common example is when a customer calls a company and is provided with a recording of top-level choices: choose number one for sales; number two for service; number three for support; and so on. Then the customer receives multiple layers in a seemingly never-ending descending spiral to get to the right person. (When I encounter these situations, I get so frustrated I just keep hitting the "0" multiple times on the phone until someone answers). While this multiple-choice system may promote internal efficiencies for the company they result in absolute frustration for the client. This is important to consider when implementing any change. Customers desire:

- Efficient turnaround times in work, callbacks, and correspondence.
- Front foot activity from the company. They do not want to have to chase.
- Helpfulness and going the extra mile, particularly in resolutions.
- Ease in dealing with the business.
- Clarity and transparency so they know what is happening at any point in the process.
- To feel like they are the only customer that matters in the moment.

I facilitated a training program for an organization's scheduling and administration team, to help them with their customer communication skills. The training came about because of the managing director's intense desire to focus on the customer first. As the team discussed what was paramount to the customer, changes were then made to work standards and processes along with how to communicate to different personalities via e-mail and phone. They started with the customer first and then worked backward from there.

Some years back I was developing a block of land and had registered my application with a local council. I had submitted my paperwork and could get no sensible answer from the staff as to why it was being delayed. I thought I'd tackle it head on and drove to the council offices. I eventually managed to speak to the officer who authorized the subdivision approvals and he told me there were two stages for approval. The first one had been completed but was still waiting for the second approval. He showed me the tray behind him where my application was sitting. I asked him who the person was that had approved the first part of the application and he told me it was him. I then asked him who it was that approved the second part. He told me it was him and no other requirements were outstanding. I looked at him incredulously and asked why he hadn't approved both sections at once. He told me it was their process. Go figure!!!

In seeking to create a lean operation through streamlined processes, sometimes the customer is forgotten and the process becomes the end in itself as Amazon founder and CEO Jeff Bezos so clearly states:

> Good process serves you so you can serve customers. But if you're not watchful, the process can become the thing. This can happen very easily in large organizations. The process becomes the proxy for the result you want. You stop looking at outcomes and just make sure you're doing the process right. Gulp. (Bezos 1997)

Reflection Point

- What specific expectations do your customers have of you?
- What needs to change to meet these expectations?
- Does your process hinder or help your clients?

Creating Lean and Streamlined Processes

1. Problem Identification and Underlying Causes

Creating lean workflows involves the identification of what areas most require improvement or correction. If we looked across our organization, we could potentially list a multitude of areas we would like to correct. They typically fall into two categories. The first is the obvious improvements: those we are conscious of and have generally caught our attention through poor results, general chaos, a deviation from the current norm, or those that fall short of the ideal. The second are those areas that are adversely impacting the achievement of our strategic purpose and related objectives and sometimes, these are harder to identify unless we as leaders have a regular time set aside for strategic review and reflection.

Once the improvement area has been identified and before proceeding with a change initiative it is necessary to investigate potential root causes, for what we may perceive as the surface problem may be caused by other underlying sources.

I consulted with a company where chaos was reigning supreme, evidenced by multiple fires burning on different fronts. Cash flow was tight; the happiness factor of the administrative team had disappeared; job errors were increasing; customer complaints were on the rise; and the broader employee base was disgruntled. When you're a *fixer* like I am, the immediate reaction is to jump in and, of course, try to fix things. However, I have learned to step back from the fires, process the issue, and ask the question, "what or who is causing this?" While the immediate reaction is to put the fire out instantly, if the cause is not corrected, the fire relights in no time. I met with the business owner and worked through each area that required attention, seeking to identify the cause, for, in this way, we would understand more accurately where the improvement initiative was required. Through the process, it became clear all the *chaos fires* had been lit by one person—the related supervisor. I subsequently met with him explaining the issues that were taking place, and it seemed that all roads were leading back to him. His response was telling. He told me the reason he was in the role was out of loyalty to the business owner. He had stepped up into the supervisory position but was over it and just wanted to do a normal job without all the responsibility. Within a week we adjusted his role, covered the supervisory position with someone else, and over subsequent weeks, the fires started to subside. The point here is the systems and workflows were all performing perfectly requiring no attention whatsoever. It was the underlying cause, the supervisor that was causing the chaos.

Not all improvement corrections are this easy but at the heart of it is locating the cause and bringing correction at that point. In their book, *The Rational Manager*, authors Charles H. Kepner and Benjamin B. Tregoe offer a six-stage process for cause identification. It is in descending order.[1]

1. What is the situation?
2. What are the problems?
3. What is the priority problem?
4. What are the possible causes?
5. What is the most likely cause?
6. What specific corrective action needs to be taken?

Explaining the above process, they say:

Problem analysis is the logical process of narrowing down a body of information during the search for a solution. At each stage, specific information relevant to the problem drops out as the process moves successively from the overall situation to what is wrong within it, then to the most important problem to be treated, then to the possible things that might have caused it to go wrong, and finally to the most likely cause. Locating this cause makes it possible to take a specific, effective action on the problem. (Tregoe and Kepner 1967, p. 19)

While we typically get sucked into putting out surface fires, finding the unseen firelighter—whether they be people or process related—is critical in the identification process.

Tracking Flow to Identify the Cause

Workflows are essentially traffic flows, just as we would see, for example, on Google maps. We enter our starting point along with the destination. When we view the map, we observe where congestion is taking place and where normal speeds are occurring, providing us with an estimated time of arrival. On this visual map overview, we immediately see where the potential problems are en route. Workflow mapping follows the same principle and the congestion map, as illustrated in Figure 5.1, helps us identify and direct us to potential underlying causes. This is particularly helpful if you are working with a team where each can engage in the visual and transformative process.

The scenario in the figure is a company that conducts electrical and plumbing repairs for its domestic customers. Cash flow is a current challenge with their average debtor days sitting at 36.

When completing the congestion map, the process follows this order.

1. Map the current process from start to finish as it is happening now.
2. On the left-hand side, indicate the ideal goal. This serves to continue prompting the question "how can we achieve this?" as we explore the current situation and delays.
3. Out to the right, we then document the current status using our best guess as to approximate time frames and issues. As this

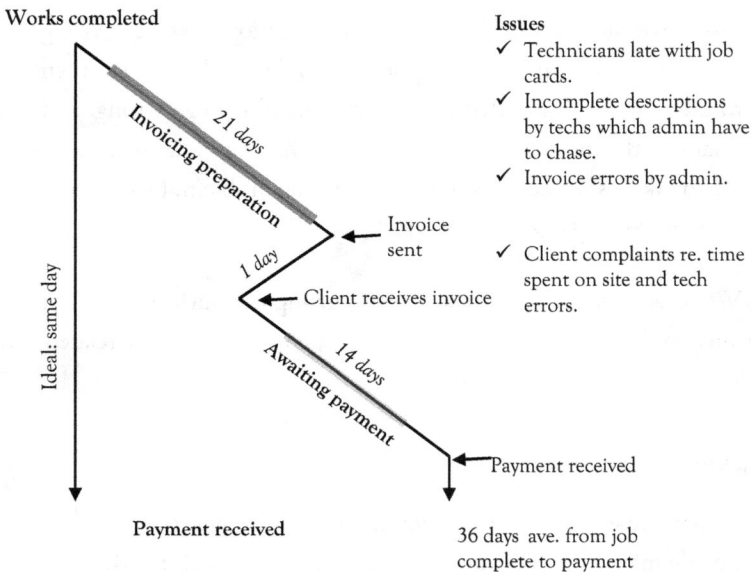

Figure 5.1 The congestion map

is drawn, the likely problems are entered along the delay paths, highlighted in red.

4. Document the customer's interaction with the organization.
5. As the problems are entered, always be asking "why is this happening?" as this assists in arriving at likely causes.

From the insight we gain through drawing the congestion map, with the questions we ask, and the deliberations of possible causes, we now have something factual to work with, even though we have not as yet validated the findings. We have broken down each of the stages with their various issues and approximate time frames. Depending on the situation, we can go directly to solution implementation or, if required, validate the current findings and from the actual data then remap the process to achieve our ideal goal. Congestion maps are useful for both micro process flows (as per the scenario above) or they can be completed at a macro-level, outlining the full flow from the initial customer order through to delivery and payment, dependent on the situation.

On one improvement project, I mapped the process from the initial inquiry through to when the salesperson met with the prospective customer. It involved tracking a piece of paper. The receptionist would write the nature of the inquiry on a piece of paper, walk over, and place it in the relevant salesperson's tray. When they eventually scheduled a meeting with the potential buyer, they would write the details on the note and put it back in the receptionist's tray. She would then update those notes into the customer relationship management system. In this process, we discovered some of the following.

- Technology was being underutilized.
- Lack of clarity in the process flow.
- No procedural guidance.
- No time frame metrics or accountability.
- Outdated way of performing work.

The company had operated this way for many years and even with the installation of a new CRM system, they continued to work in previous patterns. The time frame delays upfront, from the inquiry to a sales meeting, were excessive, and thus, performing a simple workflow analysis highlighted the obstructions throughout the process.

The other useful tool I developed to capture more specific processes (that are being completed by individuals at the various process phases) is the workflow process table, as per Table 5.1. Instead of the bigger picture approach of the congestion map (as previously shown in Figure 5.1), this process table is more detailed in the identification of steps involved and often highlights where problems are occurring. It can also be a useful validation tool in some situations. I have used a two-stage process that demonstrates the progression from one stage to another.

Completing Table 5.1 daily for two weeks provides reliable data to compile time averages and identify recurring issues. The data provides a factual account of this particular process providing substance and validation to start the change process. You will notice the technicians are the suspected cause of the problems. If we used the six-stage process of problem solving by Kepner and Tregoe (as previously mentioned in this chapter) we could identify the following:

1. The Situation. Invoices are taking too long, thus affecting cash flow.
2. Problems. Incomplete data from technicians. The assistant is too soft on the follow-up with technicians. Too many customers call regarding their invoices.
3. Priority problem. Technicians.
4. Possible causes. Technicians are overbooked, thus creating their slow responses. Laziness and disregard for the administration team's work are also possible.
5. Most likely cause. Laziness and disregard for the administration team's work.
6. Specific corrective action. Training is required for job card completion along with supervisors to now be responsible for their daily collection and submission to the office, thus increasing technicians' accountabilities. Divisional managers to hold supervisors to account for this change and the ongoing results.

Table 5.1 The workflow process table

Stage	Who	Process steps	Time (minutes)	Day	Customer interaction	Notes
Job card collation	Administrative assistant	Collect job cards from tech's tray and sort	22	1		
		Follow up techs for outstanding job cards	33	1		29% of cards for yesterday were not submitted
		Review yesterday's job cards for invoicing, highlighting errors and omissions	17	1		45% were not complete
		Call the related techs for information	75	1		Most have to call me back which takes an average of 7 days to complete information for handover to invoicing
Invoicing	Administrator	Enter job card data into MYOB	6	7		6 minutes per job card
		Customer requests re. when the invoice will be received	2	7	Customer called	Ave. of three calls per day

2. Validation

Validation before embarking on an improvement initiative helps confirm our assumptions or it helps lead us to where and what the real issues are.

A general manager was struggling with the number of hours she was having to devote to ensuring that invoices, before being sent to clients, were correct. This, along with customer complaints concerning invoicing errors, was the situational effect. We assumed it was the administrative assistant, responsible for invoicing, who was the problem. However, the other possibility was that the information she was receiving from the technicians (before invoicing) could also be the primary issue. We weren't absolutely sure so we decided to validate our assumptions, first on her invoicing involvement. Reviewing all invoices over two weeks we discovered that yes, the administrative assistant was the problem, and had a 16 percent error rate. Subsequently meeting with her I found that while there were a few upstream issues from the technicians submitting the job cards (which could be dealt with later), my major finding was she was a more expressive, big picture, fast-paced behavioral style. While she was a delightfully fun person and wanted to get a lot of work completed quickly, this particular invoicing task called for a more detailed, moderately paced behavioral style. As she was a highly valued employee and there was no other suitable position for her at the present time within the organization, I worked with her style[2] and incorporated procedural changes to the conversion process. Within a week the immediate improvement was 7 percent and then proceeded to improve further still. Validation not only confirmed the situation but then led us to the cause which enabled us to bring specific correction.

Other common causes identified through validation have been:

- Poor planning.
- Poor training.
- Reactive work styles.
- No performance metrics, process/time frame standards, or accountability.
- Targeting the wrong prospects through marketing efforts.
- Lack of communication between project managers.
- Wrong people operating in the wrong roles.

- Process duplications and lack of procedural clarity.
- Lack of role clarity between employees.
- Selling to customers who don't have the buying authority.
- Clunky technology.
- Leadership issues.

One of the valuable by-products of involving individual employees in the validation process is it helps them see their role and responsibilities at a more objective level, thus sharpening their efficiency throughout the process. And while they may feel they are under scrutiny, they often view management's request for assistance as to their importance in the organization which then promotes their own sense of value and higher levels of engagement.

3. Remapping the Process

Reverting to our original goal when we completed the initial congestion map in Figure 5.1, we desired to get same-day payment. It was a depressing meeting when we drew out the map and realized the many issues that were taking place. "How can we get money in faster?" the boss asks his administration team. One of the juniors bravely speaks up and suggests that when the client calls to book in their job, the scheduler should advise them that payment is to be made on the day. She then suggests that the technician, once they have completed the work, creates an invoice, have the client sign it, and make payment prior to departure. Thinking this might work, the team then remaps the original process to see how it would look.

The scenario in the process remap in Table 5.2 is amazingly simple and many companies are collecting same-day payment with the advance of technology. But many are still operating under the original invoicing system. I have purposefully provided this scenario, not only because it is still relatively common but it demonstrates that if we start with what seems to be an unachievable goal, those goals then evoke the *how do we make this happen* question, leading us to possible solutions. The remap then becomes the framework by which we use to start the process of planning and implementation.

Table 5.2 The process remap

Stage	Who	Process steps	Ave. time (minutes)	Day	Customer interaction
Scheduling	Scheduler	Book in job with client	5	1	Call for a technician
		Advise payment is to be made at job's completion			
Invoicing	Technician	Technician creates invoice at end of the job	10	1	
Payment	Customer	Client to sign off and make payment	5	1	Job review; signing of invoice; payment

4. Implementation and the Baseline

Once we have identified the precise area that requires correction, it then becomes a matter of choosing the best approach to initiate the change implementation. A foundational question in the process is: To arrive at our destination point in the easiest, fastest, and most cost-effective way, what options should we consider?

Related questions worth asking are:

- What are the associated costs and likely return on investment?
- From the approaches available to us, what is likely to yield the greatest benefit, and in which areas are those benefits likely to be?
- What peripheral areas will be impacted by the changes, both positively and negatively?
- What are the metrics we will use to ascertain if the changes are having the desired effect?
- Who will be our *change agent* and what resources will they require?
- What are the milestones that will indicate progress toward the desired outcome?
- What could go wrong?

Settling in for what I assumed was to be a lengthy meeting with the owner of an engineering company, we started mapping out the current production workflow as there were serious delays in work completion which was affecting profitability. After 45 minutes I stopped and said there was no point in going further. I pointed to one of the congestion lines which involved the production manager and related processes and told him if we correct that area we would get the desired results. We initiated the improvements immediately and within four months the owner reported a 65 percent increase in job completions. While there were many choices, this one thing was staring us in the face, was the easiest to implement, and was the core *en route blockage* to increase workflows. Another business owner wanted more sales. In reviewing the sales processes they were using I came to understand there were too many unqualified buyers coming through the pipeline. These were taking too much of the company's time (effectively blocking flow), with the qualified buyers being negatively impacted by the associated *unqualified load*. While some of the related processes needed streamlining, I told him to qualify the buyer on the initial phone call by asking what their budget was. While he looked slightly horrified by my recommendation, he subsequently acted on it and reported back that it was this one change that was having the most impact. Sometimes, it can be the smallest of changes that has the largest influence.

Once the course of correction has been decided upon, establishing a baseline at this point becomes important as it will provide the understanding and insight as to whether the improvements and actions we are making are having the desired effect.

An accountancy firm that had lost their way in the previous eight years and found themselves on a stubborn immovable plateau enlisted my help to shift their situation. At the start of the project, we mapped the current flow, found the congestion points and blockages, and then listed eight vital indicators to monitor throughout our work together. I wanted to ensure that as we implemented changes, they were having the desired effect and if there was any negative impact, we could make *just in time* changes. We created a spreadsheet to capture the particular baseline performance indicators to measure their current status, the improvement goal with the provision for monthly updates to record the results as the initiative progressed as per Table 5.3.

Table 5.3 Baseline indicator improvement chart

Indicator	Current status	Improvement goal	June	July
Ave. time from customer request to job start	15 days	7 days	14 days	12 days
Ave. time from job start to completion	28 days	14 days	25 days	21 days
Billable % of Accountant <NAME>	59%	85%	65%	70%

The result from clearing the blockages in workflows, technology, and personnel role changes produced a staggering 234 percent profit increase over the seven months we worked together.

The other benefit of using this baseline data method is that team members, when involved in the process through suggestions, problem identification, data collation, and ongoing tracking, are often drawn powerfully into the central flow of the change initiative and thus the broader organization. Their involvement also provides management with ground floor insights and helps each person more fully *own* the changes they have to make. The fact that employees are even listened to can be its own driving force in the change initiative.

5. Evaluation, Course Changes, and Stickability

In the accounting firm example I mentioned above, data was captured weekly, with a regular management meeting scheduled to review progress. The meeting incorporated those who were assigned tasks the previous week to understand their insights and reflections into what was working, what was not, discussion on positive and negative peripheral effects, and then required changes for the coming week.

While we do our best to create changes that address the core issues, and while it is always advisable to run *what if* scenarios to assess potential upsides and to mitigate risk, things sometimes do not go to plan. And this is why ongoing correction needs to be monitored and evaluated against the baseline. As part of the changes, we might combine four steps completed by three people, into one person responsible for all four processes, but the effect might be overwhelming for the employee. Are they the right person for the job? Is there other technology that can be utilized? Are outcomes improving against the original baseline or has there been a decline? Or a company might have reduced its six sales territories covered by six account managers to the same territory being covered by only three managers. While this makes sense to reduce overheads of sales personnel while increasing personal outputs, we notice that customer orders are delayed by two days with an increasing number of complaints in the last four weeks, something we had not anticipated. If we are not monitoring the changes against the baseline and making changes as we proceed, things can rapidly decline.

Improvement initiatives can also be short lived, partially delivering the results we had anticipated due to not staying the course over the full project. Some of the reasons for aborting early are:

- The initial changes and results are occurring too slowly.
- Not having fully ascertained the potential outcomes from the *full* change process management settles for early rewards.
- Spontaneous work styles from management impeding a more thorough, methodical process.
- The unsettledness and frustration emanating from team members who perceive the changes as negative. Fear is often the driver of these behaviors.
- Not having fully calculated the cost.

But staying the course can lead to other possibilities.

A cleaning company asked me to assist in streamlining their people and processes as they were experiencing various levels of disorder and delays in certain areas. Many adjustments were made and one of those changes created a setback, previously factored into the change initiative. Invoicing, which was being achieved within five days of a project's completion (using their paper-based system), experienced a sharp decline upon the integration of new technology which seriously affected cash flow. We had assessed the risk and understood that in the long term, the benefits across multiple areas in the business would be significant. The managing director stayed the course with invoicing and cash flow returning to normal as previously calculated. As part of the project, I had also rerouted numerous tasks away from her to other employees. As the various changes started to integrate and flow, and with a clearer mind from the alleviation of many of her previous responsibilities, she began to see a new growth horizon. In the subsequent year and with some further modification to her role, she began focusing on business development. Because she had committed to seeing the change initiative completed in its entirety, staying the course through the cash flow downturn eventuated in substantial revenue growth the following year. This would never have happened if she had aborted the process early.

6. Documentation

As the change initiative proceeds and a new way of operating is established, documenting the revised procedures, checklists, internal standards, and the shifts in people's roles is essential for embedding the new way of operating and ensuring future consistency. Some team members are excellent at remembering the first explanation of process changes while others keep asking the same questions repeatedly. Some team members are on the front foot with customer resolutions while others do not exhibit the same sense of urgency, thus an inconsistent experience for the client. Documentation in these areas helps provide this consistency while pushing responsibility back on employees to access the information themselves rather than taking up management's time in asking questions. The other advantage is maintaining uniformity when employees are absent, whether on temporary leave or depart the organization entirely. It means the new person in the role can quickly follow standardized processes and checklists to assist in duplicating expected outputs. Documentation provides ease of transition while providing consistency to internal workflows and customer expectations.

Reflection Point

- Looking across your organization, where are the most noticeable inefficiencies?
- From your observations, which one of these areas, if improved, would yield significant returns?
- How will you implement your findings from this point?

Summary

Waste through inefficiency is hiding everywhere. Rather than jumping straight into putting out fires, find the firelighter, the root cause. When we understand the true nature of the problem it is important to:

- Consider customer impact, ensuring it is a positive one.
- Validate our assumptions.
- Use a mapping process as a means to further identifying issues, gaining team member contribution and insights throughout the exercise.
- Remap the process in light of the ideal situation.
- Pull the trigger on a change initiative while ensuring we have a data baseline to measure all subsequent changes against.
- Manage the change process, make corrections as required, and update all documentation.
- Stay the course.

Developing a lean operation through efficient workflows yields significant and often dramatic returns to those who are willing to embrace the process and go the distance. A constant focus on eliminating waste enables the organization to do *more with less*, thus driving our competitive advantage.

Endnotes

1. (Tregoe and Kepner 1967, p. 19).
2. I have found in my coaching work that it is impossible to make someone who they are not. To expect someone to operate in their opposite social/ behavioral style, which in this illustration is from fast to slow, from expressive to analytical, is pointless. I have observed, however, that by working with a person's style and implementing certain processes and checklists into their work, while supporting and coaching them in those changes, assists in causing a behavioral *stretch* which often achieves what is required.

CHAPTER 6

Marketing

A Targeted Approach
Always Wins the Day

Game Changer: *Efficient marketing is about taking our message directly to where our ideal buyer will meet us.*

I recently moved into a new home and decided I would purchase some equipment to complete my hi-fi system. The Facebook marketplace has become a favorite platform for purchasing high-quality items at a fraction of the new price so I started my research, found a set of perfect bookshelf speakers, and bought them. Throughout my time of research, I noticed that other bookshelf speakers and related hi-fi components were appearing, unrequested, from retail stores in other cities. From my Facebook activity and broader web searches, I had obviously been identified as a potential buyer with a particular requirement and was marketed to accordingly.

This example demonstrates some of the central elements of efficient marketing: identifying and understanding our potential buyer; the specific (product) wants and needs of the buyer; the most effective channel or medium for our message to appear; and then the timing of such. But before we can take a specific marketing aim, gaining insight into our core business is crucial.

Core Business

I worked with the third-generation owner of a construction company in Sydney that built a variety of products: garden sheds, carports, patios, residential homes, and large industrial sheds. They were well known for quality work but the economy was down, prices had dropped, and multiple competitors had moved into their space, particularly in the garden sheds, patios, and carport products they provided. Sales revenues had been dramatically affected in recent times and part of our work together was to turn this around. Instead of initially ramping up their marketing efforts, I wanted to ensure that the products they were taking to market passed three foundational aspects.

1. They demonstrated high expertise in the construction of the relevant products.
2. It was meaningful and enjoyable work for them.
3. It was profitable work with an understanding of what products made the greatest margins.

The assessment of these three areas revealed there was a significant division. On one side of the divide were the garden sheds, patios, and carports. These were not profitable; they disliked doing this particular work but were proficient in the construction of them. The other insight that arose was the competition who had moved into their city was focused on these three offerings as well, thus creating a cut-throat pricing war, driving profitability down while creating large volumes of price-sensitive shoppers. While we could have reviewed their buying and production costs to become more competitive, they simply weren't enthusiastic about it. However, on the other side, the residential homes and industrial sheds passed all three areas with a resounding *yes*. The margins were significant, there was a sense of purpose and enjoyment in the work, and they were highly skilled at it. The assessment model is demonstrated in Figure 6.1.

Gaining insight into these three areas enabled us to understand which of these products should be marketed to their potential buyers and those that should be stopped completely. From this initial assessment, I reviewed all facets of their current marketing to ascertain what shifts were required moving forward with the most memorable observation being their radio advertising. Ninety-five percent of the advertisement marketed carports, garden sheds, and patios—the three products that had failed the core

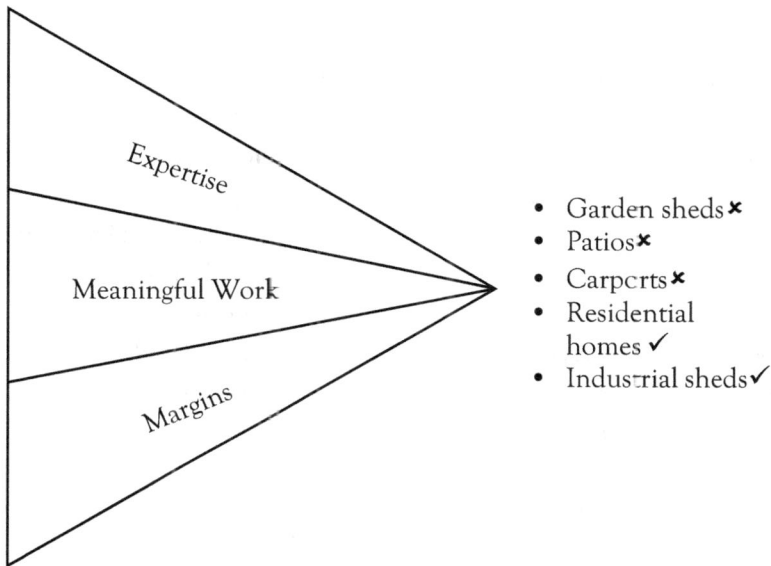

Figure 6.1 Core business analysis

business analysis. While the advertisement made the phone ring, the calls were not for their high profit and meaningful work, and nor did they represent the ideal buyer identity.

Efficient marketing isn't just about the effectiveness of our promotion and having people enquire or purchase our products. It's also about ensuring that what we are marketing is feeding back to the organization a sense of purpose fulfillment, the opportunity to work in areas that we are proficient in, while representing significant profit.

There is a caveat though. If, as part of our strategic directive (as outlined in Chapter 2), products are identified as *loss leaders*—those unprofitable products that initially cause customers to buy from us that then, in turn, create more business from those same customers from higher profit products—then these have their place.

Reflection Point

- What products are you selling that fail the expertise, meaningful work, and margin model?

Who Is Your Ideal Buyer?

Consider two fishers, one a novice and one experienced. The novice heads out to sea with little preparation and no understanding of the type of fish they are wanting to catch. Dropping their line randomly in different locations, their impatience makes for a disheartening day catching little for their efforts. The experienced fisher on the other hand knows the specific types of fish they are after. They have studied them; understand the places they are likely to be; have the appropriate tackle, bait, or lure; and exercise patient persistence. They build on their knowledge over time of what works and what doesn't and then, with this knowledge, become more effective in their craft. And efficient marketing exhibits the traits of this experienced fisher. Instead of random and ad hoc approaches, we understand the specifics of our prospective customers and market to them in a way that provokes interest and increases the chances of gaining them as clients. The greater our understanding of them, the more specific we can be in meeting their needs and marketing effectively.

The Buyer Identity Profile

There are two main areas to consider when seeking to build an identity profile on our prospective customers. The first is demographics and the second is psychographics.

Demographics are the more tangible or concrete aspects of who the buyer is. These consist of such areas as age, gender, occupation, income, race, religion, family size, education, and location. Psychographics focuses on the more intangible psychological aspects of the person which includes personality, attitudes and assumptions, interests, values, activities, needs, the problems they face, and their goals. Both aspects are important in the creation of the identity profile as they assist in the understanding of *who* the person is and *why* they are likely to buy. It provides us with the knowledge of *who* to go in the first instance and then help us in tailoring our marketing messaging and then the subsequent sales process to connect to their *why*. Table 6.1 provides an outline of this process which you can complete on one of your current customer types.

Most organizations have different types of buyers, thus segmentation is important in the consideration of our marketing efficiency. Armed with

Table 6.1 Buyer identity profile

Buyer identity			
Demographics		Psychographics	
Age		Personality	
Gender		Attitudes	
Occupation		Assumptions	
Income		Interests	
Race		Values	
Religion		Activities	
Family		Needs	
Education		Problems	
Location		Goals	

the knowledge of the buyer identity, two other considerations require mentioning. The first is who authorizes the final purchase, and second, who the influencers are.

Decision Makers and Influencers

I finally learned the importance of marketing to the decision maker—those who authorize the purchase—the hard way. Flying six hours across the country and arriving at an introductory meeting with the managing director of an earthmoving company, we began discussing the issues they were having and the solutions I could bring. Twenty minutes into the meeting I realized that in my initial marketing call to this company I hadn't adequately determined who the decision maker was. I knew his wife happened to work in the business and upon probing for the purchasing process he said "well yes, my wife will be involved in the decision as well." As she was not available and I was unable to change my return flight, I made an appointment for the following week with both of them. I eventually won the project, but it took an additional 20 hours with a significant financial cost, due to my failure of ascertaining who the *real* buyer was.

A company I consulted had several products they marketed to their customers. We analyzed the quotes that had converted to sales and, as part of the analysis, we listed the distance of the person (who the quote was submitted to) from the decision maker. It was clear that marketing conversations and the subsequent quotes being submitted were often two or three levels down from the actual person who authorized the project. The person at level three would submit the quote to the person at level two who, in turn, would submit the quote to buyer one, the decision maker. From this insight, the business owner redirected his focus to meeting with the decision makers, winning three projects in the subsequent two months that he would have been unlikely to win previously. Targeting the actual decision maker is an important element in driving our marketing efficiencies and saves waste (as I personally found out) in the process.

The other persons of interest in marketing messaging are the influencers. Influencers are those who recommend our products to the purchaser. It might be children who, seeing a toy or an ice cream, tug on mum's arm persuasively explaining why they *really* need it. Or the teenager who sees a new gaming platform his friends are gravitating to and presents their case to the parents. A mid-level manager, who has been reading management articles by a certain authority, recommends an upcoming seminar to their boss. Our products can be marketed to these influencers who hold the persuasive power in recommendations to the purchaser. They are an often forgotten target in our marketing but are worth considering when taking our message to the marketplace.

Reflection Point

- When you take your product to the marketplace, who would you consider the real buyer to be?
- Who are those influencers that you need to be mindful of and target in your marketing efforts?

What Are You Really Selling?

"You stink," one person said to another. "You need to go and see Blueline Dry Cleaners." This radio advertisement immediately caught my attention. A normal dry cleaning company, with a large number of competitors, distinguished themselves in just one brief conversation. While their business is dry cleaning, they are selling *stink-free living*. Dentists often sell *smiles*; a hardware chain in Australia sells *lowest prices*; BMW sells *sheer driving pleasure*; an electrical contractor sells *connecting you to the future*, while a property developer sells *enduring value*. When I was a mortgage broker, my message was *helping you get ahead* and now as a consultant, I sell *driving organizational efficiency*. The message we convey to prospective customers can be drawn from the underlying business model that appeals to the potential buyer or it can be driven by our sense of purpose and what we are most passionate about. Our message must resonate with our potential customers and clearly portray the benefits when they purchase our products and become part of our customer communities.

Reflection Point

- What are you really selling and define it in a few words?

Going to the Intersection

Just as the experienced fisher knows the particular fish they are wanting to catch, understands the likely places they will find them, and then drops their line or net at the location, so too with efficient marketing. Knowing who our ideal buyer is, where they shop, what appeals to them, and the places they are likely to be helps us more precisely drive our message to those specific intersections where potential buyers meet our business, as per Figure 6.2.

Figure 6.2 Core business and buyer intersection

The key to meeting our potential buyers at the intersection is about identifying which particular marketing platforms and methods are the most likely interaction points.

One to One

One to one marketing is where the business typically takes their message to one potential customer at a time. This can include:

- Targeted advertising where our products appear in the customer's line of sight.
- Direct e-mail, messages, and snail mail.
- Requesting specific referrals.
- Calling our prospective buyers directly.
- Sending books or articles to a potential buyer with a follow-up phone call.

One to Some

One to some is where the business may have multiple buyer types and for which they need to take a broader approach. Take, for example, a local independent wine shop. They sell to a variety of age groups, ethnic origins, experience levels from the connoisseur down to the beginner, and so on. To increase the market's awareness of the products they sell they might use:

- Social media advertising to their specific buyer identities.
- Targeted events for their current customers and friends.
- Wine education nights where prospective buyers are likely to attend.
- Article writing for publications their buyers are likely to read.
- Regular e-mails and blogs sent to their contact lists.
- Advertisements in local papers, magazines, and trade journals.
- Attendance at networking events.

One to Many

One to many typically belongs to those organizations whose product is used by multiple buyer identities and who continually need to hold their brand high above marketplace noise. Amazon, Coca-Cola Amatil, and Apple fit into this category. Methods here might include:

- Billboards.
- Radio and television.
- Online banner advertising.
- Targeted social media campaigns and advertisement placements.
- Sponsorships and events.

Sometimes, a combination of the above is used. In my business, while *one to one* is the most utilized and effective method, I use *one to some* for broader lead generation and brand awareness, but it is still focused on going to the intersection where my ideal buyers are likely to be. My *one to some* includes speaking at workshops and keynote speeches, facilitating webinars, posting on LinkedIn and Twitter, and article publications in relevant trade journals. The trap many small- and mid-size companies fall into is the employment of some or all of these with an ad hoc, hoping we hit something approach, rather than a focused systematic plan based on the core business and ideal buyer identity.

Reflection Point

- How can you more efficiently take your message to the intersection where potential buyers will find you?

Results Evaluation and Tactical Adjustments

Evaluating the effects of our marketing is a process that is often overlooked in the pursuit of getting our message to the intersection. We are busy making it happen on the front end but fail to understand what is happening on the back end.

An efficient marketing analysis follows a repeated two-stage process, as shown in Figure 6.3. This drives progress upwards as we evaluate results from our current marketing efforts, make tactical adjustments from our insights, evaluate those changes, and continue the same process.

Instead of a random point, shoot, and hope method, taking the time to evaluate what is working, what is not, and then adjust our tactics based on our evaluation continue to sharpen our effectiveness and increase results. Even when our current methods are having the desired effect, why stop there? If we took what is working and then made small adjustments, and evaluated the effect of those changes, we can find that previous expectations and satisfaction levels had been too low. Where our adjustments show no signs of improvement, or where they have undesired results, it is then necessary to revert to what we were previously doing and then try something different, evaluating the results again to ascertain whether there has been an improvement. When we continue this process, we continue to drive our marketing efficiency on an ever-ascending scale.

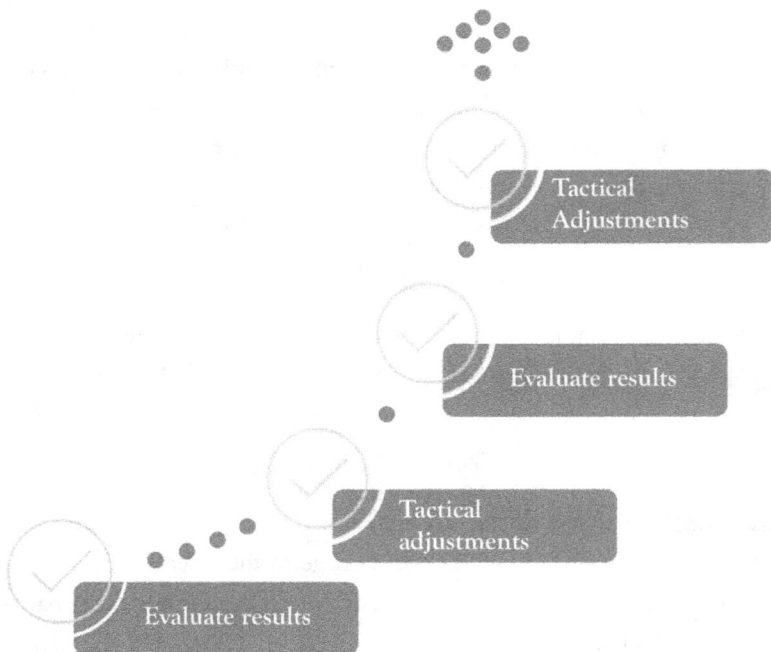

Figure 6.3 Marketing analysis process

What to Evaluate

The following are some of the areas to consider when conducting evaluation.

- Numbers of inquiries.
- Source of inquiries, for example, Google search, LinkedIn.
- Number of and cost of inquiry per marketing source.
- Return on advertising spend.
- Cost per client acquisition.
- Qualified leads resulting from inquiries.
- Resultant sales per source of inquiry or platform.
- Accuracy of buyer identity and core business target_ng.
- Headlines and content effectiveness.
- Are the inquiries aligned with the strategic direction?

It is not necessary to analyze all of these, but it serves as an idea of what is possible and the list is by no means exhaustive. The failure of many organizations is when something is working, they rest at that point, never realizing if they evaluated their current marketing and then continued making tactical adjustments they could be significant.y further along with increasing qualified inquiries with decreased effort and financial outlay in the process.

When They Come, Look after Them

I mentioned in Chapter 5 the priority of understanding customer impact when considering the effect of streamlining internal workflow process. In seeking to create a lean operation that eliminates unnecessary overheads, rationalizes workforces according to seasonal loading and customer demand, and automating as much as possible, sometimes, the potential buyer, when they do come from our marketing efforts, does not get taken care of. If the potential buyer feels they are not welcomed or cared for in the process, they end up going elsewhere. Our marketing budget, spent on enticing them to our door, is wasted as they walk back out the door, empty handed.

Organizations would do well to take a customer-centric approach as opposed to a profit-centric approach. While profitability .s important for those who represent *for profit* enterprises, when bottom-line results are the primary focus with customers being second (or often further down the ladder), the internal focus becomes a never-ending descending spiral of cost control and customer dissatisfaction. For some reason, we forget that customers spend money and the more they are looked after the more they will spend with us. Amazon is a great example of this and as of November 21, 2020, they had the following mentioned on their jobs website:

> Our mission is to be Earth's most customer-centric company. This is what unites Amazonians across teams and geographies as we are all striving to delight our customers and make their lives easier, one innovative product, service, and idea at a time.

While it is easy to document a customer-centric value such as Amazon's, it is a whole other matter to deliver. If a customer-first approach is indeed a purposeful and heartfelt focus, then we can work backward from there to establish efficient systems to serve the customer while being mindful of profitability impacts.

Here are some considerations on how to ensure that people are feeling the love when they interact with your organization.

- Avoid the mistake of employing *task-oriented* people for customer-oriented roles. Many hotels and restaurants make this mistake.
- Ensure staffing numbers are adequate so that customers get looked after in a timely manner.
- Ensure the environment, whether actual or virtual makes the customer feel welcome. A restaurant that turns its air conditioners off in winter to save costs or an online platform that is difficult to use causes people to think twice about the initial transaction or returning to these businesses for a second time.
- Train your people how to effectively communicate and care. This needs to happen in all forms of communication whether face-to-face, e-mail, phone, or online messaging services.

- Ensure there is the transparency of data in a unified system that relevant people have access to and can relay information to the customer immediately.
- Automated messages and e-mails are ideal for keeping the customer in the loop but break down when they feel they are being held at arm's length or their inquiry is not being responded to specifically.
- Customer service teams need to be educated that while there are templates to use to respond to customer inquiries, a few extra seconds taken to read incoming mail *properly* is wise. This way the individual can decide what the best response to the customer should be.
- All incoming inquiries need to be responded to in a timely manner. This necessitates standardized and documented turnaround time frames.
- Use Customer Relationship Management tools to capture incoming inquiries and ensure that each person involved in the *inquiry to sale process* is both using it and updating it. Otherwise, it is too easy for inquiries to slip through the cracks.
- Ask your customers if there is anything you could be doing better for them.
- Teach your people not to avoid customer conflict or blame someone else for their complaint. Front foot immediacy and honesty will always win the day.

Delighting customers and making their lives easier. A powerful driver of business performance that causes us to review every aspect of our organizations.

Reflection Point

- Is your customer central to your organization and if so, how would you validate this?
- In what ways can you improve the customer experience?

Referrals. Good News Spreads Fast, Bad News Even Faster

A major outcome of providing exceptional service to every inquiry and our current customers is that they, in turn, sing our praises. And when someone calls because they want what their friend has, most times these represent our ideal buyer with the added bonus of being no cost of acquisition. At one time, if we didn't return a customer's phone call promptly, if we didn't follow through on what we said we'd do, and if we did appalling work, the negative impact was constrained to the client's immediate circle and the outer perimeters of that network. That was bad enough. These days, in our connected global village, good news travels fast but bad news ... can circulate the globe in no time at all. And while many provide excellent products and world-class workmanship, their tardy responsiveness to inquiries and client requests along with slow product delivery in the absence of timely communication results in situations as portrayed in Figure 6.4.[1]

In my previous finance business, I was interested to see where my inquiries and resulting work was coming from and who was *feeding* me. As I crunched the numbers it became glaringly apparent that my top 20 percent of clients were all multiproperty investors with a majority of referral business coming directly from them. This top tier, while representing where most of my revenue was derived from, also represented my core business—my expertise, meaningful work, and high margins. I decided to trial *preferential treatment*. I began holding events specifically for these clients with the content aligned to their specific interests and values, the psychographic element of their buyer identity. While it was my way of saying thank you to these customers it also fuelled repeat business and created significant referral momentum. This was in many ways an informal membership in a platinum club where my top clients could receive high value while also connecting with others who shared the common interest of property investment.

This form of referral business is what can be considered as unsolicited. We don't ask for the referrals, but they are a by-product of good work and high customer value—the result of good news spreading fast. Another part of referral business is that of *solicited* referrals where we specifically ask a current client or someone we know for a direct introduction to another. High-performing insurance salespeople have often built their success on this method.

Figure 6.4 Not the best referral

"Who do you know who could do with the type of assistance I provide?"

"Could you provide me the names of three people to whom I could introduce myself and my work to?"

"I notice from your LinkedIn profile that you know James from Smith Corp. Would you be able to introduce us both?"

I called a business owner recently that came from a solicited referral and said, "John mentioned I should call you. He said you're a good guy, you run a good business and we should meet." He laughed, the conversation was warm from the start and we booked a time to meet. When we cold call, the first stage is creating interest and attempting to build a connection which is a difficult process, accompanied by low sale conversion ratios. But when asking for a specific referral from someone we know, we generally enter a warm situation where building rapport and trust is fast tracked.

Diverse Pathways and Consistency

I often ask businesses what their marketing approaches are and sometimes they will proudly say that all their business comes from word of mouth, so they don't have to do any other form of marketing. While this is a wonderful situation to be in, it is a risk to be fully reliant on word of mouth business: given changing economies—the COVID-19 pandemic is a classic case of a dramatic and fast-negative impact on the sales for many businesses; the nature of hungry competitors; internal errors and poor workmanship adversely affecting our customers and so forth. If we simply rely on word of mouth it may be that, at some stage, the phone will go quiet.

Designing a marketing plan with multiple avenues to generate inquiries creates consistency throughout, and if one source dries up, there are others still in process that continue generating inquiries. Where one method is relied upon only, or when there is inconsistency in our marketing efforts, the classic peak and trough scenario comes into play—we have too much work at the peaks and not enough in our troughs. These rises and falls make for challenging workflow and inventory planning along with the organization of appropriate staffing numbers. Consistent marketing through multiple avenues, on the other hand, helps smooth out these peaks and troughs enabling us to plan our backend operations more effectively. The other reason for such inconsistent inquiries is that often, when things are busy, our marketing activity slows, sometimes to a stop. Then, when that busy period has been completed, we realize there is a lack of upcoming work and we crank up the marketing wheel once again to drive more inquiries to win more work, and thus the peak to trough cycle continues. Consistency with multiple approaches will always win the day.

Efficient marketing is also about making the most of every single qualified inquiry and then keeping in front of them until they decide to buy or they no longer want to be connected.

At one time, I needed some painting completed for my home. I called a painter; he came and gave me a quote. I decided not to proceed with the painting at that time but a year later I was ready. I couldn't find his quote nor his business card and he had never bothered to keep in touch. I subsequently called another painter and gave my business to them. Around the same time, I called a plumbing company to fix some leaking taps. They arrived, completed the job, and within a week, I received a thank you letter along with some discount vouchers for my next job, which I used. Then, I received their regular monthly e-mail. That was 10 years ago and to this day, I still receive their monthly updates and their name is *top of mind*.

The painter: never followed up, never kept in touch, and never received my work.

The plumber: constantly reminds me they are there for any future work I require.

The plumber demonstrates brilliantly that excellent workmanship combined with an initial marketing approach to entice me back for my next job (through their discount vouchers), along with staying in front of me through their monthly newsletter, will help drive consistency in their job requests.

Some years ago I was involved in a national roadshow speaking to 11 audiences. At the conclusion of my speech, I asked the business owners in the room how many of them sent a regular newsletter to all their current and past clients along with anyone who had made contact with their company. Less than 5 percent indicated affirmatively with some of the audiences being 1 percent. This one method, sending a monthly newsletter combined with regular social media posts, will help you gain a *front of mind* position and when the time comes, you will be the first they call. It doesn't take much to be in the top 5 percent and despite all the e-mail traffic we receive these days, if you educate people about your offerings, providing content of high value (as opposed to just selling your products), you may find your newsletters and the social media presence are highly effective in bringing consistency of inquiries.

The acquisition of new customers can be a costly exercise. If we were focused on staying in front of our existing and past clients along with every contact that is made through our marketing effort; kept in front of them by occasional calls, e-mails, social media posts, and special events; followed up each inquiry and quotation with diligence and focus: these and more would assist in mitigating the sales troughs so often experienced. Marketing should be happening all the time through multiple avenues, not just when we need more sales.

Reflection Point

- What areas in your marketing approaches could do with a higher level of consistency?
- What content could you provide by way of a newsletter or social media posts to inform and educate your audience?

Summary

Efficient marketing is:

- Understanding our core business—what we are proficient in, that which is meaningful to us and represents profitable products and work.
- Identifying our buyer identities.
- Identifying what we are *really* selling and marketing this message to our particular buyer identities.
- Going direct as possible and meeting them at the intersection, where buyer meets seller.
- Respecting every inquiry with a central focus of care for the customer.
- Consistency with multiple marketing approaches.
- Always seeking to be front of mind with our customers and prospects.

In a crowded business environment where many compete for the same customers, ensuring we are *front of mind,* while making it easy for prospective customers to buy when they do come, elevates our competitive advantage given that many organizations fail in this critical area.

Endnote

1. (Hodge, Smash The Bottleneck 2015, p. 24).

CHAPTER 7

Sales

It's All about Process, Not Personality

Game Changer: *When we understand that everyone can sell, despite what personality they possess, and then integrate efficient sales processes with evaluation, course correction, and team training, sales effectiveness dramatically improves.*

When I went into business some 20 years ago, I recall my brother asking me how I was ever going to do well in business, highlighting my quietness and reserved nature. I wondered at the time if he might be right. I had come across other extroverted salespeople who seemed to be infectious in their enthusiasm and appeared they could talk all day. Other books I read and seminars I attended at the time also highlighted the need to be an exciting and vivacious salesperson. I was doomed or so I thought. But then, I came across a piece of text by sales guru Tom Hopkins who said:

> When it comes to great salespeople, I will take an *interested introvert over* an *interesting extrovert every* time. While it may be true that interesting extroverts are the life of the party, drawing others around them, it's the interested introverts who make others feel important … who gain their trust. And trust creates the environment for sales. (Hopkins 2012)

Those words provided hope to this introvert and ultimately supercharged my sales effectiveness.

Why Everyone Can Sell

From the moment we are born, we request what we want and need. A newborn automatically asks for its mother's milk. As children, if we wanted something, we asked for it. And when the answer to our request was *no*, it didn't stop there. We learned to surmount the *no* for a possible *yes*. Then, as we progressed into adulthood, we persuaded employers to hire us; people to date us; our favorite to marry us; sellers to lower their prices on items we wanted to buy; hotel staff for upgrades; and mothers-in-law to like us. These persuasion events happen daily and are the language of influence. While none of these examples is selling in the traditional sense of a financial transaction, they are what we would call nonsales selling.[1]

A survey commissioned by Daniel Pink called *What Do You Do at Work?* (with data collated from an adjusted sample of more than 7,000 adult full-time workers in the United States) found that about 40 percent of people's time in the workplace involved nonsales selling. One major finding that emerged was:

> People are now spending about 40 percent of their time at work engaged in non-sales selling—persuading, influencing, and convincing others in ways that don't involve anyone making a purchase. Across a range of professions, we are devoting roughly twenty-four minutes of every hour to moving others. (Pink 2012, p. 21)

Persuading, influencing, and convincing others. The language of humanity. If we view traditional transactional selling through the lens of influence—where we are *influencing others for mutually beneficial outcomes*—this then offers a change in perspective. Extrovert, introvert, or ambivert: wherever we are on the personality scale, when we frame selling as *positively contributing to another's betterment*, then all of us can achieve this in the traditional sense of sales.

The Heart of Sales

At the heart of sales is the person, both the company representative and the prospective buyer. One of the reasons that selling is often seen as manipulative is the perception of it being a one-way street where the salesperson is cajoling us into parting with our money. We feel they are just in it to make a dime without taking into consideration who we are and what we need. They're only interested in themselves and in these situations, we feel exploited. The true nature of sales is one of *mutually beneficial outcomes*, where the salesperson wins from the transaction along with the buyer having their needs or wants met. In this way, both parties win. And for this to take place, the salesperson must be interested in *what is best for the buyer* and if the product they are selling is not in the buyer's best interest, then the salesperson communicates this accordingly. We can be schooled in the best sales techniques and learn our scripts by rote, but if a prospective customer senses the lack of care in them as a person, they will soon depart our presence. Being interested in providing significant value to others along with significant value back to our organization is where we get these *mutually beneficial outcomes.*

Why Process Is Needed

Given all of us are intrinsically *wired* to influence others independent of personality, having a sales process to follow then becomes foundational to efficient selling. No longer is the domain of sales left to the extrovert but becomes accessible to everyone.

Railway carriages require tracks to move ahead, keeping them advancing toward their preset destination. And just like the rail track, sales tracks are required to keep both the salesperson and the prospective customer moving toward the destination of closing the sale or, what I like to think of is, welcoming a new customer into our community. When there is no sales track, extreme sales inefficiencies can be the result.

The Sales Track

Laying out a sales track for everyone within our business to follow helps drive sales forward in a consistent and efficient manner. The following example is a simplified sales track with the corresponding process prompts and questions, where quotations are issued as part of the buying process.

1. **Qualification**
   - What do they need? (basic level)
   - What is their budget?

- When do they require this?
- Who is the decision maker?

2. **Needs identification**
   - What do they need? (detailed level)
   - Discuss the best solution.
   - Clarify the budget again.
   - Schedule meeting to complete quotation. *The decision maker must be in attendance.*

3. **Quotation meeting**
   - Clarify all previous conversations and document onto the proposal template.
   - Ensure you capture what it means to them personally, why they want/need this.
   - Mention you will provide some options on the quote.
   - Communicate when they will receive the quotation.
   - Schedule a follow-up call.

4. **Quote follow-up/sales completion**
   Call as scheduled and ask:
   - Does the quote reflect our discussions and what you require?
   - If no: make amendments, resend quote, and schedule another follow-up call.
   - If yes, ask which option they would prefer.
   - Provide options for start dates and schedule time accordingly.
   - Provide options for payment.

In the above example, four stages standardize the process for each company representative to follow, along with key questions and prompts. When a sales track is in place with the relevant training for team members, it mitigates the emphasis on personality types.

Reflection Point

- Map your particular sales track in Table 7.1, listing the various stages along with one question or prompt that is important in your sales process.

Table 7.1 Sales process track

Stage	Key question/prompt

Making It Easy for Buyers to Buy

When people seek us out to explore the purchase of our products, they want it made easy, free of obstacles. Potential buyers often come armed with knowledge from their prior research and want us to guide them in the most efficient manner to get what they want or need. Or, if it is an online purchase, the ease of the web platform needs to be seamless, otherwise, people will go elsewhere. When it is an in-person sales transaction, taking an interest in *who* the person is, while asking pertinent questions upfront, arms us with *buyer knowledge* enabling us to build rapport, fill in the knowledge gaps, and head straight to solutions. From the organization's side, a predesigned sales track ensures we are streamlining the process for the buyer. Otherwise, if the whole sales process is left to random intuitive guidance from the representative, it can frustrate buyers with no one winning in the process.

Leading with Questions

One of the reasons for sales inefficiency is the representative talking too much. When we talk too much, we miss what is important to the potential buyer in front of us. Leading with questions helps us understand their knowledge and requirements and assist the representative to fill in the gaps, leading the buyer from start to finish in a smooth process. Questions can be designed to elicit yes or no responses or can be used for providing options. These help us understand the buyer's engagement, desire, and readiness to buy.

"This will take about 15 minutes for me to demonstrate this. Does that work for you?"

"Are you happy with what you have seen thus far?"

"Do you think your family will enjoy this when it is in your lounge room?"

"Does this proposal reflect what you are wanting?"

These questions are designed to elicit a yes or no. The *yes* confirms the buyer is on track with what you are proposing, with the *no* indicating a switch of tracks is possibly required. A *no* can also indicate they are researching or just browsing as opposed to having an immediate intention to buy.

But questions eliciting a *no* response can also be designed to ascertain a *yes,* their readiness to buy.

"You mentioned you have been doing this for several years now without results. If you don't change the way you are approaching this, do you think anything will change?" "No."

"From your research, have you seen anything else as good as this machine in front of you?" "No."

Questions can also be framed in terms of options.

"This model comes in black, blue, and white. Which color would you prefer?"

"Out of these three banks, which would suit your requirements best?"

"As you mentioned one of the places you'd like to visit is Europe, this week we have specials on Italy and France and we also have an amazing deal for Austria. Which one of those countries interest you most?"

When options are used it is no longer in the realm of yes or no, but *which one should they choose*. It also makes it efficient for the buyer. When the representative is leading with options it makes it much easier for the buyer to decide, speeding up the process for both parties and, in the case where no options are suitable, the representative can make a swift track change to ensure they have heard the buyer correctly and to reposition things accordingly. Options are also important for online decisions. Instead of having only one choice, many companies now offer several options at different price points, for example, hardback, softcover, or Kindle version, in the case of book sales. This again transitions the decision-making process from *should I buy this or not?* to *which one should I choose?*

In the sales track example I used earlier in this chapter, there were four main stages: (1) qualification, (2) needs identification, (3) quotation meeting, (4) quote follow-up/sales completion. Each of these stages can have their tailored *option* questions for the representative to ask throughout the process. Here are some examples.

1. Qualification
   "This kind of home comes at three different price points. $250,000, $375,000, or $500,000 or, we can custom design something for you within that price range. Out of these, which would suit your budget?"

2. Needs identification
   "You mentioned earlier your sales volumes have plummeted. I find this generally relates to broader market influences, internal sales people, or poor sales management. Which one of those would it relate to and are there others more pertinent?"

3. Quotation meeting
   "I can prepare this quotation and have it to you within 24 hours. I'd like to call you to ensure it reflects what you are requiring. Would Thursday morning or Friday afternoon work best for a call?"

4. Quote follow-up/sales completion
   "Will you be paying by cash or credit card?"

Reflection Point

- List some yes and no questions you could use in your process.
- List some option questions that you could also use.

Personality. The Inverse of What Most Salespeople Think

Many years ago, I was accredited for a behavioral profiling system known as DiSC. I met with the accreditation officer late one afternoon over a drink at a luxury hotel in downtown Brisbane with the meeting designed to ensure I knew the profiling process along with its origins. Within minutes I felt like I had met my new best friend. When I was upbeat, he was too. When I took pauses, he gave me space. When I laughed he laughed. He engaged with me exactly where I was in the moment. As I walked out of the hotel, I reflected on how much I liked the guy. As soon as that thought crossed my mind, I realized the reason I liked him was because he was *just like me.*

When we consider the people we want to spend time with, they often share similar traits and interests to us, and these connect us. In sales situations, we often do not have the luxury of getting to know the potential buyer over a lengthy period of time and we generally don't get to choose the people who show up interested in our offerings. This is where learning to build rapid rapport is essential. Once rapport is built, people are more likely to trust which provides a solid foundation for effective selling as demonstrated in Figure 7.1.

One of the many benefits of understanding behavioral or social styles (I covered this in detail in Chapter 4) is when we flex our style to match that of another person, rapport can happen rapidly, as it did for me with the accreditation officer. And this is what many people in sales neglect.

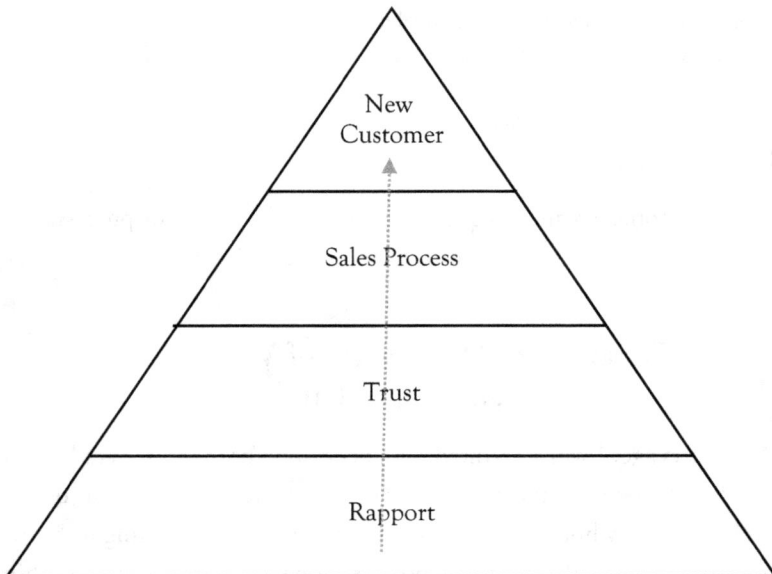

Figure 7.1 Foundations of rapport and trust

In failing to rapidly build rapport, trust is difficult to establish and where there is no trust, generally there is no sale. Building rapport quickly comes from style adaption along with being interested in the other person and what is important to them. This foundation of rapport becomes advantageous to both buyer and seller making the sales process more efficient and increasing the chances of gaining a new customer.

Several years back I rushed into a store to purchase a television and a salesperson asked if he could help. My objectives were to check if they had the size I needed, the picture clarity, how much it was, and when it could be delivered. I would have bought it on the spot. However, the salesperson started on a technical rant, proceeding to explain all the specifications that made this particular television exceptional. I immediately felt tired and left without making a purchase. This story illustrates what happens when we fail to flex to the customer's style and preferences. While my buying process contained only four objectives, his process seemed infinite. I was focused on (dare I say it) the big picture; he went into detail. I wanted to be in and out of there with a television within 10 minutes. He seemed happy to talk all day. Rapport wasn't built and he lost the sale.

Personality is important but it is the buyer's personality that takes precedence, not the salesperson. If the customer wants detail, we provide detail. If they are expressive and want to tell us about their recent holiday, how drunk they got last night, or their visit to grandma's farm we go for the round the world journey with them. If the person is indecisive and painstakingly slow, we move at a gentle pace with them and if they just want the fast facts then that is what we provide.

The salesperson's responsibility is to adapt their style to match the buyer's style and when we combine this with taking a genuine interest in the buyer, new customers are created faster and in greater numbers.

Underlying Personal Value Drivers

In a sales training session I conducted with a small team, I asked the attendees about their clients and what was important to them, beyond the actual products they were buying. The team identified areas such as safety; the accuracy of specifications; to be held in high regard by senior management (which had deeper importance of future job security); and then ease of decision making. These areas were the underlying personal drivers of value that caused these clients to buy.

At one time I was looking to purchase a luxury car. I went to a BMW showroom and the salesperson was exceptional. He found out what was important to me in my decision-making process, provided *only* the necessary information I required and then took me over to one of the cars I was interested in and invited me to take the driver's seat. As I sat in the car, he looked at me and smiling said, "you look cool in this car." I must confess, I bought the car. While this admission makes me wince somewhat, the BMW representative had the insight to go beyond the actual product to what was driving my buying decision. I wanted to be seen by others as successful, and *cool* was part of that equation.

Value drivers are those underlying motivations that drive the buying decision and are a powerful force in the sales process. And this is why leading with questions is so important. When we as the seller talk too much, we miss the subtle nuances that hint at what is driving the buying decision whereas, when the buyer is doing the majority of the talking, it is easier to ascertain these motivations. Consider the underlying value driver examples in Table 7.2.

Each of the situations highlights that while the buyer might state the initial reason for their purchase, underlying that reason is a motivation driving the buying decision. This is where the astute sales representative understands that the stated reason to purchase is often in the domain of the rational. It is the logical and conscious decision for the buyer, however, emotion is what moves them, and the more effective we are at uncovering these underlying drivers, the higher our sales volumes will be.

Table 7.2 Underlying value drivers

Product	Stated purchase reason	Underlying value drivers examples
Investment property	Grow their wealth	Future security
Bookkeeping	Keep on top of finances	Control
Consulting	Increase revenues	Decreased stress
Interior furnishings	Upgrade their home	Social recognition
Overseas holiday	Need a break	Freedom

Table 7.3 Current client value drivers identification

Name	Stated purchase reason	Possible value drivers

Reflection Point

- In Table 7.3, make a list of three current prospects or customers you are currently working with. See if you can recall the conversations you have had with them to ascertain what their value drivers might be.

Product Benefit Drivers

Closely aligned with internal value drivers is that of product benefits. When we establish the value of what we are selling in light of how the buyer benefits, it makes the buying decision all that much easier.

When I was refinancing people's mortgages, I would create a spreadsheet with three different lenders demonstrating the interest savings over the next 3, 5, and 10 years. When people realized that by refinancing for a cost of $5,000 now, but over the next 10 years they would save $100,000, the rationale of the decision was plain as day. The benefits far outweighed the associated refinancing costs. When we fail to reach an agreement with a buyer, one of the reasons is they have not seen enough value to make the decision to purchase. When the value is not discussed or documented the buyer effectively views the purchase as a cost as opposed to an investment. In the case of the refinancing example, the client would have seen the $5,000 refinancing cost in isolation, but when they see the benefit of $100,000, the cost becomes relative to the value received, making the decision easier.

The benefits or value to the buyer can be both tangible and intangible. Tangible or actual benefits are those that can be more effectively measured. They might include:

- Current costs of inefficiencies.
- Potential expenditure savings.

- Turnover or net profit increases.
- More time with the family.
- Better health.

Intangible or indeterminate benefits are those more difficult to measure but nevertheless add weight to the benefits of the purchasing decision. These might include:

- A more harmonious workplace.
- Decreased stress.
- Increased control.
- Better standing with peers.
- Higher self-esteem.

As the sales representative, it is important to uncover these benefits, specific to the buyer. In this way, each sales conversation or quotation moves from being generic to specific, from being seen as a cost to an investment. If the benefits are great enough, the price becomes secondary.

Keeping Records to Fast Track Improvements

Frank Bettger, author of *How I Raised Myself from Failure to Success in Selling* said, "Without records, we have no way of knowing what we are doing wrong. I can get more inspiration of studying my own records, than anything I can read in a magazine."[2] When I first read this some 20 years ago, I determined to do likewise and have since been astounded that most salespeople I've met neglect to keep records of their sales work. While many companies have internal data on numbers and conversion ratios, this rarely gets reviewed and if it does, it is rarely translated into incremental improvement initiatives with individual sales personnel or sales teams.

As an example, for those who are involved in face-to-face sales meetings the records that can be collated are:

- Number of referrals received.
- Number of calls made.

- Number of meetings made.
- Number of meetings kept.
- Number of proposal meetings.
- Number of sales.
- Dollar value of sales.
- Source of sales. These might be from existing clients, referrals, cold calls, and so on.

A related ratio summary sheet can also be established to gather the data into categories such as:

- Calls to appointments.
- Appointments to proposals.
- Proposals to sales.

Keeping records provides an accountability process to the sales manager, team, and individual representative. Rather than meandering one's way through a week, updating daily progress helps hold the salesperson *in-line* to both corporate expectations and personal standards.

Whether we have in-store or field salespeople the process is the same, just modified accordingly. For example, if I were selling perfume as a shop assistant I would want to know my effectiveness with genders; age ranges; number of people I spoke to; subsequent people who purchased; product take-up; average and total dollar sales value. I would also test out different customer approaches. For one week I might use the dreadful "are you happy just browsing?" line. I would then try "was there something specific you came in to look for today?" I would analyze those numbers against the original script to ascertain if it were more effective. I might then try "thank you for coming into our shop today. Tell me, what are your favorite notes or characteristics you enjoy in perfume?" I would then test that against the others and in this way, I am continually improving my effectiveness.

And when we do collect data, instead of it sitting untouched in *the cloud* we must use it to improve our condition on the ground. In analyzing a construction company, I discovered one of the estimators (who was involved in the sales process) had a 7 percent conversion rate, from estimates to sales. The business owner was astounded by how low the percentage was and, to his credit, immediately made changes. It is one thing to have the data, which they had been keeping, but quite another to review the data and trial different methods to increase sales effectiveness. Sales left to chance are opportunities gone to waste.

Letting the Fish off the Hook.
Objections and Rebuttals

Prospective buyers object all the time and we should be concerned if they do not have some form of objection. Objections are expressions of interest for if they are not interested, there is nothing to object to. Objections generally mean someone has or is considering your proposition, their mind is engaged and thinking through it, and they see some potential hurdle to the purchase. Whether it is an in-store sales person selling mobile phones or a construction company taking months to prepare and bid on a new project, to get to the decision point with the buyer and then have the sale not proceed due to an objection we were not prepared for amounts to negligence. Preparation, in understanding the common objections you receive along with knowing how to respond to overcome those objections, drives efficiency for both buyer and seller.

Responses or rebuttals are designed to overcome objections through the presentation of sound reasoning. Our response to an objection is often best in the form of a question (or a statement that elicits a question from the buyer) because questions keep the discussion open and moving toward the sales decision.

I met with a business owner about a potential new project and after learning the price they objected that it *cost too much*. My response was a statement: "That's exactly why you need me." Looking surprised they immediately asked, "what makes you say that?" I went on to say that given they had been in business for 20 years and still could not afford my fees demonstrated they needed my help. Sound reasoning through a logical response won the project.

Over a two-year period, I had been, at various times, in discussions with a business owner about doing a new project with them. I had got to know them quite well given the number of meetings and calls we had together. They agreed to discuss the project again and as the decision point came, they started to object. It wasn't the right time, they thought they should do it on their own and it cost too much. I then made a statement: "From knowing you as I do, I perceive you to be a very intuitive person." "Yes, you would be correct in that," they responded. I then asked, "what is your intuition telling you about working with me on this project?" to which they answered, "my intuition is telling me I can trust you and we should do this." We booked a start time for the project and worked together for the following two years. I was convinced this business owner would gain significant value from working with me, but I had to find a way to overcome the multitude of objections they had thrown my way. I never let them off the hook.

Objections, while numerous, generally fall into five categories:

1. Authority.
2. Money.
3. Time.
4. Trust (credibility of the company or salesperson).
5. Suitability.

In Table 7.4, I have provided an example of both an objection and a corresponding rebuttal.

Being well prepared with rebuttals to the objections we receive results in mutually beneficial outcomes where both the buyer and the organization win.

Reflection Point

- List some of the common objections you receive and then write a relevant rebuttal for each of them.

Table 7.4 Common objections and rebuttals

Objection	Rebuttal
Time	
It's not the right time for me at present	When would be the right time?
When things slow down, we could look at doing this then	Some of my best clients implemented this project when they were busy and they found that …
Money	
I can't afford it	You had mentioned earlier this was in your budget range. What has changed since then?
	Instead of one upfront payment, would it be easier to make four payments over the next 6 months?
Authority	
I must talk it over with my partner	How about we make a time to discuss this with them? I'm available tomorrow afternoon or Wednesday morning. Which of those would suit you best?
Trust	
I'm not sure your company can deliver on this in the time frame we need it completed by	What makes you say that?
Suitability	
I don't like that color. I was hoping for a blue one	What if we could get it in blue for you and have it delivered next week?

Summary

Sales efficiency is about:

- Having the foundational belief that all of us can sell.
- Demonstrating a deep interest in the potential buyer as a person.
- Making it easy for buyers to buy.
- Designing a sales track and following that process.
- Understanding the need to adapt to the different social styles of the buyer.
- Uncovering personal value drivers.
- Demonstrating product benefits and value.

- Keeping records of progress, always seeking to increase our effectiveness.
- To be well rehearsed and prepared with rebuttals to all common objections that come our way.

Endnotes

1. The term Non-Sales selling is credited to Daniel Pink from his exceptional book, *To Sell is Human*.
2. (Bettger 1979, p. 14).

CHAPTER 8

Money

"I Think We're Doing Ok"
Is Just Not Good Enough

Game Changer: *It is too easy for organizations to get caught up in the pursuit of growth and doing the work, without paying attention to their financials. But those who rely on financial data as the basis for all expenditure, growth, and investment decisions operate with greater clarity and foresight. This in turn significantly enhances organizational efficiencies.*

As there are volumes covering financial literacy, I will not deal with these aspects in this brief chapter but rather, from observations and work in this field, discuss the more common financial issues that either give rise to, or are the result of, financial inefficiencies.

When our finances are not given the due respect and time required, it impacts efficiencies and financial outcomes in ways we often underestimate: too many unproductive people; excess inventory; low job and product profitability; unwarranted overheads; cash trickle rather than cash flow. Financial issues result in time waste and increased stress for management and just the stress alone is enough to take the focus away from driving a business forward, ensuring it is efficient throughout and gaining competitive advantage. Some of the strongest and most profitable privately held organizations I have worked with have been owned by those who have never been trained in finance nor do they want to be. However, these business owners understand how critical financial management is, and, compensating for their knowledge deficiency, employ people with strong financial management skills along with external financial advisors.

Frequency of Advice

One major observation I have made is that those who involve their financial managers and external advisors on a frequent basis tend to do better than those who do not. Apart from the quality of the advice is the frequency of advice that helps dramatically. For example, many meet with their external accountants annually, for the purpose of tax planning and a review of the year's performance. While tax planning and reviews are necessary, it is the frequency that is critical. If a company only meets with their external advisor annually and one month after their review there is a negative financial impact that goes undetected, this could have serious consequences in the subsequent 11 months. But if they had been having monthly reviews and analysis, they would have managed to make *just in time* changes, intercepting the increasing losses. Whether you have in-house financial management, external advisors, or a combination of both, consistent review of the data is crucial to enable effective decision making. Frequent advice from smart people is the smart thing to do.

Forecasting

The owner of a pipe manufacturing business was explaining they were going through a short-term downturn in work. When I asked them about how they were positioned financially for the next few months they responded with, "I think we should be okay." I then asked if that comment was based on forecasting or gut feel. It was the latter, and, in my opinion, this is not good enough and leaves that company vulnerable to failure.

Forecasts are a *casting forward* of future projections, created from data that represent a *reliable* and anticipated expectation. For instance, if a company has grown consistently by 20 percent year on year, we could assume this data is dependable. However, if the previous quarter or year's revenue doubled due to one major client's purchase, we would consider that a one-off situation and use the periods prior. While forecasting lies more in the predictive realm, forecasts provide tremendous clarity for budgetary allocation and the timing of expenditure decisions. When utilized, decision making is no longer assigned to the realm of *gut feel* or the amount of cash we have at hand but rather, every decision is in accordance with a carefully and well-thought through forecast.

A construction firm had been operating with constant financial ambiguity for many years, basing their decisions on cash at hand, receivables and payables along with the due dates for work in progress claims. While the managing director received these reports on a regular basis it was still difficult to make decisions, particularly in downturns or when they had to outlay significant cash to start new construction projects. As part of my work with them, I implemented a 12-month cash flow forecast that was updated weekly from the accounts department. The director came into the office one day carrying the forecast and said, "This is one of the best things I have ever had. For the first time, I can see what is happening." This forecast delivered a *stress freedom*, providing him with the knowledge of when to spend and when not to, when to hold back and when to release, and a greater amount of energy to continue driving the business forward rather than being constantly worried about the future.

Cash flow forecasting is a powerful tool, not only from the perspective of being able to see the coming weeks and months but that can also be used in conjunction with our business planning and resource investments. One company I was working with was deliberating with employing the services of another supervisor. The decision was made easier when we entered his employment costs and estimated revenue increase (from an allocation of a percentage of his time to billable hours) into the forecast, immediately clarifying that yes, this was a sound financial decision. Another company was growing phenomenally, doubling every six months which presented an ongoing cash challenge for the owner. Cash flow forecasting assisted in managing the growth along with advanced understanding of when the shortfalls were anticipated. This provided a warning light in advance to then navigate the flow of cash more efficiently through these periods.

Cash flow forecasting is also extremely useful when managing our creditors. At various times we experience cash delays and shortfalls which then affect the timeliness of our payments to those we owe money to. Using a forecast to input the timing of these payments, based on the flow of cash, with proactive communication to the creditor with the date they can expect payment, alleviates their angst and intercepts the potential rise in incoming calls through these periods. Management fails when they put their head in the sand, don't forecast, don't return creditor calls, and just wait for the situation to right itself.

When Profits Hide Losses

Reviewing the financial reports with a business owner it appeared that all divisions of their company were extremely profitable. As we conversed, I enquired into one of the divisions reporting methods and discovered that within that one division, there were two very distinct departments managed by two separate leaders with teams under their leadership. From this insight, I requested a historical report on the profitability of both areas and it clearly demonstrated that one of the departments was extremely profitable with the other experiencing ongoing losses. The way the existing reporting had been created covered up the fact that profit in one department was hiding the losses in the other. With this knowledge, we were then able to focus on returning it to break even over the following six months and then to a profitable status thereafter. Obtaining clear profitability separation of each department, service offering, and product, combined with regular review and analysis, provides the platform for managing costs and increasing profitability where possible.

This also applies where companies are more project or service based in their work as opposed to the sale of individual products. One of the failures I often see is that each job is not reviewed at its completion to ascertain its profitability but rather, if the company is showing a profit at year end, then all is well with the world. Job completion analysis is important as it highlights what worked well and what did not; where it was efficient and where there were cost overruns along with where the actuals exceeded budget in terms of materials and labor hours. These reviews can be tremendously useful in continuing to improve ongoing efficiencies and the resulting profitability. Whether jobs are shown to be profitable or have experienced losses, reviewing performance and productivity in all associated areas makes us sharper on every new job we quote on and complete. Without this, we are merely hoping that everyone did what was expected, the budget was adequate, and we made some money along the way.

Margin Benchmarks

An owner of a business brought me in to increase sales volumes and wanted me to devise attractive commission structures to recruit high-performing sales people. While all this sounded great at the top level, the company had been experiencing ongoing losses for a significant period of time and when I broached this with the owner, he firmly told me that more sales would dig him out of the hole he was in, thus the reason he needed my help. Before going any further, I analyzed every job they had completed in the previous six months and saw that the majority of them had made a loss. I told him that until we corrected the profitability margins on all future work, it would be pointless to get any more sales. He looked confused. I went on to say that if I increased his sales, I was only going to increase his losses. He didn't appreciate my opinion, so we parted company.

Another company I worked with was smart. The directors had established a margin benchmark for all their work and armed with a report, one of the directors met weekly with the various managers to discuss the previous week's jobs. Every job that was below the benchmark was reviewed to identify where the potential fail points were. This kept the manager focused and accountable for their work while continuing to sharpen the pricing process and underlying work efficiencies to increasingly meet or exceed this margin benchmark.

Personnel Productivity

In Chapter 5, I mentioned an accounting firm that experienced a 234 percent profit increase from an improvement initiative we completed. Part of that financial upsurge came from the harnessing of their employees' attention and personal efficiencies toward their individual and collective output targets. It was not an ad hoc approach but rather an intentional focus with corresponding accountabilities.

Financial pain or limited financial gains are often the results of management not clearly defining these expectations and outputs with a lack of awareness of where time waste and inattention are taking place. I read a frequency collection report from the supplier to a small trade services business I was consulting to. The data showed the staff who were billed out by the hour were traveling to the supplier on average 6.34 times per day which was the result of inadequate planning and no accountability. We estimated the revenue loss to be in excess of $80 thousand dollars per annum. It does not take much to lose much.

I was consulting through a significant upturn in the Coal Seam Gas industry and, due to the expansionary opportunities, many of the contracting companies grew exponentially in a short space of time. This growth explosion necessitated recruiting new people to fill newly created roles. I noticed that as new people were added to the organization, the productivity and performance outputs of the existing employees often declined. These companies were increasing their wage expenses while at the same time losing revenue from lower productivity. That's not a great equation.

In a recent article published in the *Australian Financial Review*, Stewart Butterfield, cofounder and chief executive of the software giant Slack, says he would love to avoid the mistake of hiring too many people, and "what frightens him most about this prospect are the challenges of remaining nimble and productive." He also says he is "trying to avoid having a bloated workforce, in which employees spend too much time creating work for themselves and each other."[1] Whether it is in high-growth situations or when considering hiring a new person to alleviate pressure from others, it's important to review the roles and performance of the people we already have. This along with creating greater efficiencies within systems and processes can help keep staff numbers at minimal levels while increasing their effectiveness. If companies did this regularly they would find there is often significant untapped capacity within the people they already have onboard. Wasted time is the unseen thief of revenue and profitability.

Inventory Turnover and Debtor Days

In preliminary conversations with organizations I have consulted to, cash flow is often identified as a major pain point. I recall seeing a photo of a warehouse full of pallets, each laden with piles of money, and was a graphic illustration of where cash can sit when excess stock is held. Ensuring there is tight stock control with *just in time* ordering wherever possible; arranging with suppliers to return unused materials; organizing with sellers to deliver directly to the customer while holding enough inventory ourselves to meet client demand ensure that available cash is preserved and turnover days are optimized.

Another major contributing factor to poor cash flow is inefficient debtor recovery procedures. This is where stringent financial management is crucial to ensure that when accounts go over the payment terms by as much as one day, a specific retrieval process is triggered. When this is neglected, creditors knowing they won't be chased for their outstanding payment are often happy to have the cash sit in their bank account. One company I consulted with who initially did not have this retrieval process in place had 73 percent of its accounts sitting outside of their standard payment terms, and much of this was in 90+ days. The implementation of a consistent follow-up process reduced those outstanding debtors by 97 percent with the remainder having to be written off. In my work with debtor recovery procedures and related employees, I have found that if they don't manage the process stringently and with a high level of assertiveness, creditors will play the avoidance game for as long as they can. One thing certainly holds for chasing money: *he who yells loudest wins.*

Focusing on the *One Thing* for Growth

Many who are prone to working in the details suffer from getting lost in those details. The amount of accessible data becomes a minefield of confusion, resulting in unsurety about the way forward and generally arises from not having identified the simple markers of progress. As one business owner confessed, as he placed a one-inch thick folder full of reports in front of me. "We have so much data I have no idea what to look for."

Focusing on *the one thing* can bring clarity to confusion and directs our efforts accordingly. Best Buy, Starbucks, and Limited Brands, for example, have identified the revenue value that a 0.1 percent increase in employee engagement can create, with Best Buy placing that value at $100,000.[2] Knowing this *one thing* enables clarity of focus and concentration of effort into increasing engagement: the underlying factor for their revenue growth. And with this identification then comes the process of supportive planning and actions, ensuring our focus and resources are contributing directly to its fulfillment. One organization I worked with set a revenue growth goal of 25 percent for the forthcoming year. We then established the *one thing*: a dollar amount for quotations *approved* per month. We knew if quotation approvals hit this level then the goal would be achieved. Not only did they achieve the goal but hit a 32 percent increase for the year. This result did not come from clever marketing strategies, sales training, or telling people to work longer and harder. It came from identifying the *one thing*, and then, working back from there, ensuring that people's focus, time, relevant systems, and accountabilities were all a cohesive part of the plan.

Reflection Point

- From the areas covered in this chapter, what one or two areas do you need to give attention to?
- What is the *one thing* that could transform your organization's financial status?

Summary

Efficient financial management is about:

- Not leaving the financial area to chance. Instead of relying on intuition, data is relied upon for all important financial decisions.
- Ensuring frequent financial advice is part of our management responsibilities.
- Operating from budgetary and cash flow forecasting models rather than cash at hand.
- The awareness that profitability in some areas can hide losses in others.
- Ensuring our pricing and relevant margins are set appropriately.

- Confirming our existing people are highly productive before recruiting new staff.
- Being stringent on inventory management.
- Incorporating a debtor follow-up system.
- Finding the *one thing* that will positively impact your financial well-being.

Endnotes

1. (Patten 2020).
2. (Davenport 2010).

In Conclusion

When COVID-19 spread its tentacles around the globe in early 2020, the impact on business necessitated fast, decisive action from leadership. The strategy of yesterday was torn up to survive tomorrow. Within weeks of cities locking down and restricting movement, some businesses closed their doors while nimble companies pivoted: some started manufacturing new products; restaurants delivered dinner to its customers' doors; gyms and yoga studios went online; music and video platforms created new offers; and hardware stores offered curbside pickup. These companies adapted fast, letting go of some or, in many cases, all of that which had worked in the past to create a new future version of themselves. Some changes that many had been working on for the last couple of years were completed within weeks of the pandemic. This quick change of course then enabled them to gain a fresh competitive advantage over those less agile and creative. And it also taught us new ways of being efficient because we had to.

Reflecting on the contents of this book in light of the recent global changes, efficiency has meant:

- Leaders had to change their style to suit the new conditions, with many taking the Commanding General stance. It necessitated fast decision making while enlisting the full support of the troops.
- Strategic directional changes. This had to happen on the run rather than month-long deliberations in boardrooms.
- Survival tactics created singularity of focus.
- Team members had to get onboard with the changes, work together as a team, and deliver results. Those who did not, in many cases, had to be let go.
- Workflows that had previously been slow and inefficient were swiftly brought up to speed, with duplications and obstacles quickly dealt with and eradicated.

- The focus and intentionality of marketing shifted. We have learned to think differently and more creatively.
- The perspective of sales also changed with every inquiry now being seen as gold, contributing to our survival. No matter what the personality of the team member was, they all had to follow up these inquiries, sharpening their skills in the process.
- Financial management was seen to be absolutely critical. Every accountant I know says they were run off their feet with their business clients needing advice.

While lean operations in the best of times are important, when the external headwinds of change shift as quickly and dramatically as they have this past year, it demonstrates that efficiency in all organizational areas is crucial. As Plato said, "our need will be the real creator"[1] and it is this need of the current time that can be leveraged to more effectively develop lean operations for our competitive advantage. We cannot afford to do what we've always done because the game has changed and so must ours.

Endnote

1. (Plato c 375 BC).

References

Amazon. n.d. "Amazon Jobs." https://amazon.jobs/en/ (accessed November 20, 2020).

Amazon. n.d. "Amazon Jobs." https://amazon.jobs/en/working/working-amazon (accessed August 24, 2020).

Baily, M. 2020. "Arts and Culture." *Australian Financial Review.* 21 February. https://afr.com/life-and-luxury/arts-and-culture/how-guitar-genius-pat-metheny-gets-in-the-zone-20200212-p54091 (accessed September 15, 2020).

Bettger, F. 1979. *How I Raised Myself From Failure To Success In Selling.* Suffolk: Richard Clay (The Chaucer Press) Ltd.

Bezos, J. 1997. "Archives." *U.S Securities and Exchange Commission.* https://sec.gov/Archives/edgar/data/1018724/000119312517120198/d373368dex991.htm (accessed September 28, 2020).

Bolton, R., and D. Grover Bolton. 1984. *Social Style/Management Style.* New York, NY: AMACOM.

Brown, B. 2015. *Rising Strong.* New York, NY: Spiegel and Grau.

Clarkson, N. 2015. "About Virgin: Latest." https://virgin.com. 9 December. https://virgin.com/entrepreneur/richard-branson-why-delegation-crucial-success (accessed November 18, 2020).

Collins, J. 2001. *Good To Great. Why Some Companies Make the Leap...and Others Don't.* London: Random House Business Books.

Davenport, T.H., J. Harris, and J. Shapiro. 2010. "Analytics: Competing On Talent Analytics." *Harvard Business Review.* October, https://hbr.org/2010/10/competing-on-talent-analytics (accessed August 31, 2020).

Gallo, C. May 25, 2011. https://forbes.com, https://forbes.com/sites/carminegallo/2011/05/25/jfks-twitter-friendly-vision/#3272912468ce

Grandner, M.A. 2018. "The Cost of Sleep Lost: Implications for Health, Performance, and the Bottom Line." *American Journal of Health Promotion* (Sage) 32, no. 7, 1629–1634. (accessed November 18, 2020). doi: 10.1177/0890117118790621a

Harper, D. 2001–2020. "Word: Reflection." *Online Etymology Dictionary,* www.etymonline.com/word/reflection (accessed September 19, 2020).

Hodge, R. 2015. *Smash The Bottleneck.* Brisbane: Ray Hodge.

Hodge, R. 2019. "Blog." 27 November, https://rayhodge.com.au/the-expertise-teachability-model/

Hodge, R. 2019. "Blog." 4 February, www.rayhodge.com.au/task-congestion-alleviation/

Hodge, R. 2019. "Blog." *Ray Hodge website*. 27 November, https://rayhodge.com.au/the-expertise-teachability-model/ (accessed August 5, 2020).

Hollo, A. 2018. *From Impossible To Possible. Two Simple Rules To Assure Exceptional Public Value*, 2nd ed. Grammar Factory Pty Ltd.

Hopkins, T. 2012. "Blog: Tom Hopkins." 4 May. http://tomhopkins.com/blog/presentation/less-is-more (accessed August 26, 2020).

Kennedy, J.F. 1962. "John F. Kennedy Moon Speech - Rice Stadium." 12 September, https://er.jsc.nasa.gov/ https://er.jsc.nasa.gov/seh/ricetalk.htm (accessed November 20, 2020).

Kutsyuruba, B., and K.D. Walker 2016. "The Destructive Effects of Distrust: Leaders As Brokers Of Trust In Organizations." *The Dark Side of Leadership: Identifying and Overcoming Unethical Practice in Organizations (Advances in Educational Administration, Vol. 26)*. Emerald Group Publishing Limited. doi: https://doi.org/10.1108/S1479-366020160000026008

Mackenzie, A. 1990. *The Time Trap*. New York, NY: AMACOM.

Merriam-Webster, Incorporated. 1828–2020. "Dictionary: Reflection." *Merriam-Webster,* https://merriam-webster.com/dictionary/reflection#:~:text=Definition%20of%20reflection,of%20bending%20or%20folding%20back (accessed September 19, 2020).

Mitchell, T. 2014. *Essays on Life*. Glasgow: Vagabond Voices Publishing Ltd.

Pang, A.S.K. 2018. *Rest. Why You Get More Done When You Work Less*, 2nd ed. London: Penguin Life.

Patten, S. 2020. "Work and Careers: Boss." *Financial Review*. 13 November, https://afr.com/work-and-careers/leaders/why-slack-s-ceo-fears-getting-too-big-20201028-p569cf (accessed November 13, 2020).

Pietersen, W. 2016. "Von Clausewitz on War: Six Lessons for the Modern Strategist." *Columbia Business School*. 12 February, https://www8.gsb.columbia.edu/articles/node/1788/von-clausewitz-on-war-six-lessons-for-the-modern-strategist (accessed September 21, 2020).

Pink, D.H. 2012. *To Sell Is Human. The Suprising Truth About Moving Others*. London: Penguin Group.

Pink, D.H. 2018. *When: The Scientific Secrets of Perfect Timing*. Melbourne: The Text Publishing Company.

Plato. c 375 BC. *Republic*.

Rosekind, M.R., K.B. Gregory, M.M. Mallis, S.L. Brandt, B. Seal, and D. Lerner. 2010. "The Cost of Poor Sleep: Workplace Productivity Loss and Associated Costs." *Journal of Occupation and Environmental Medicine*. doi: 10.1097/JOM.0b013e3181c78c30

Rumelt, R. 2017. *Good Strategy Bad Strategy. The Difference and Why It Matters*. London: Profile Books Ltd.

Smithsonian National Air and Space Museum. n.d. "Apollo To The Moon." https://airandspace.si.edu/exhibitions/apollo-to-the-moon/online/racing-to-space/moon-decision.cfm (accessed September 21, 2020).

Taylor, A. 2020. "National: 'A Bad Apple': Mayor Rejects Claim Bondi Locals are 'A Bit Racist'." *The Sydney Morning Herald,* 21 June. https://smh.com.au/national/a-bad-apple-mayor-rejects-claim-bondi-locals-are-a-bit-racist-20200620-p554jq.html (accessed November 20, 2020).

Tracy, B. 2007. *The Art of Closing the Sale: The Key to Making More Money Faster in the World of Professional Selling.* Nashville: Thomas Nelson.

Tracy, B. n.d. "Blog: Time Management." *Brian Tracy International,* https://briantracy.com/blog/time-management/plan-ahead-and-increase-productivity/ (accessed July 11, 2020).

Tregoe, B.B., and C.H. Kepner. 1967. *The Rational Manager. A Systematic Approach to Problem Solving and Decision Making,* 2nd ed. Princeton: Kepner-Tregoe, Inc.

Tregoe, B.B., and J.W. Zimmerman. 1980. *Top Management Strategy. What It Is and How To Make It Work.* New York, NY: Simon & Schuster, Inc.

Weiss, A. 1990. *Making It Work. Turning Strategy Into Action Throughout Your Organization.* New York, NY: Harper Business.

About the Author

Ray Hodge works as a Business Advisor, Speaker, and Writer, helping organizations and their leaders dramatically improve efficiencies and gain competitive advantage. He has worked with small companies in the bush to the Department of the Prime Minister and Cabinet and much in between. Ray is a Certified Construction Professional (CCP) and the author of two other books—*Smash the Bottleneck* and *The Business of People*. He publishes frequently in trade magazines and conducts keynote speeches and workshops on efficiency and leadership. He is the coauthor of four children, is attempting to learn tango dancing from his partner Michelle, and resides in Adelaide, Australia.

Index

OTHER TITLES IN THE SUPPLY AND OPERATIONS MANAGEMENT COLLECTION

Joy M. Field, Boston College, Editor

- *Sustainable Quality* by Joseph Diele
- *Why Quality is Important and How It Applies in Diverse Business and Social Environments, Volume II* by Paul Hayes
- *Why Quality is Important and How It Applies in Diverse Business and Social Environments, Volume I* by Paul Hayes
- *The Cost* by Chris Domanski
- *The Barn Door is Open* by Serge Alfonse
- *Optimizing the Supply Chain* by Jay E. Fortenberry
- *Insightful Quality, Second Edition* by Victor E. Sower Frank K. Fair
- *Managing Using the Diamond Principle* by Mark W. Johnson
- *The Effect of Supply Chain Management on Business Performance* by Milan Frankl
- *The Global Supply Chain and Risk Management* by Stuart Rosenberg
- *Moving into the Express Lane* by Rick Pay
- *Operations Management in China* by Craig Seidelson
- *Logistics Management* by Tan Miller and Matthew J. Liberatore
- *The Practical Guide to Transforming Your Company* by Daniel Plung and Connie Krull
- *Leading and Managing Strategic Suppliers* by Richard Moxham

Concise and Applied Business Books

The Collection listed above is one of 30 business subject collections that Business Expert Press has grown to make BEP a premiere publisher of print and digital books. Our concise and applied books are for...

- Professionals and Practitioners
- Faculty who adopt our books for courses
- Librarians who know that BEP's Digital Libraries are a unique way to offer students ebooks to download, not restricted with any digital rights management
- Executive Training Course Leaders
- Business Seminar Organizers

Business Expert Press books are for anyone who needs to dig deeper on business ideas, goals, and solutions to everyday problems. Whether one print book, one ebook, or buying a digital library of 110 ebooks, we remain the affordable and smart way to be business smart. For more information, please visit www.businessexpertpress.com, or contact sales@businessexpertpress.com.

www.ingramcontent.com/pod-product-compliance
Lightning Source LLC
Chambersburg PA
CBHW061316220326

41599CB00026B/4912